Catherine Gra

À LA
TEXAS

RESTAURANT RECIPES

TEXT by
MICHAEL GRADY

PUBLISHER:
CATHERINE GRADY CRABTREE

RECIPE TESTING:
JANE EGGER

COVER ART:
LEAH LAKE-POWELL

ILLUSTRATIONS:
JAMES F. SNITILY

CRABTREE PUBLISHING

Printed in the United States of America
Published by:
CRABTREE PUBLISHING
P.O. BOX 3451
FEDERAL WAY, WASHINGTON 98063

For additional copies write directly
To Crabtree Publishing
or use order forms in back of book.
I.S.B.N. 937070-04-1

ACKNOWLEDGEMENT

Many months ago, Catherine Crabtree invited me to partici-
pate in this project. Much earlier, I had sated myself on a
similiar endeavor, A LA NEW ORLEANS, but in weighing this
recent invitation, I felt rumblings for new territory, new cuisine.
Soon preliminary materials began arriving at my door. I commenced forays into libraries and discovered the Sports Section
and Food Section now had equal billing. My gustatorial
odyssey seemed near at hand when a hurricane and certain
other difficulties set Texas on the back burner for more than
eight months.

Eventually, the pine tops of the soggy side of Texas rose to brush
the belly of my flight from Chicago. During the next eight
weeks, I flew within the state and viewed differing trees,
different terrain. I sat in the Hill Country and fed upon a
sundown. I prowled mission ruins and invited the past to come
forth and vanquish the present. I rode on the words of a
greenskeeper with a bent for Texas history. I weighed the
incongruity of a landlocked naval officer, legs deep in denim,
discussing grapes and irrigation.

But most of those days were spent with individuals who were
asked to lay their pens, menus and tasting spoons aside and
open their offices, restaurants and kitchens to the stranger with
pencil and paper. Without their cooperation, the pine tops, et
al, would not have been.

These Restaurant Owners, Chefs, Managers and Maitre d's,
Food Critics and Public Relations People, Vineyard Owners and
the Texas Department of Agriculture gave the work ethic
added dignity and represented the Lone Star in stellar fashion.

MICHAEL GRADY

And a special thanks to the following:
Jennifer Boeth
Judy Gremm
Mark Hanna
Jean Lively
Liz Logan
Nancylee Lyles
Jane Marshall
Beth Duke

NOTES FROM THE TEST KITCHEN

The chefs of Texas have submitted exciting, fun to cook recipes reflecting the state's vast areas, divergent heritages and lifestyles. How about an informal meal built around Texas Steak Salad or a Brie Omelette? For a special event you can serve Venison and Lamb with Onion Puree and a Vegetable Mousse or a Smoked Salmon Fettuccine. The dessert possibilities range from a light Bananas Cordial to a sinfully rich Sacher Torte. I urge you to try these and all the recipes in A LA TEXAS.

We have tested and retested every recipe, simplifying them if necessary so that you can prepare them easily without guess work or questions. If an ingredient is seasonal or regional, we have suggested appropriate substitutions. Terms that may be new or unfamiliar to you are defined in the Glossary.

And here's a great idea to use anytime. Sauces can turn a plain piece of meat, fish or poultry into something special. Therefore, as in the rest of our series, we have a detailed Sauce Index in the back of the book. Many take only minutes to prepare and use simple ingredients you probably have on hand. Be sure to use it. It lists Sauces for Chicken, Sauces for Fish, Sauces for Beef, etc...

Within a few minutes you can turn ordinary meals into something spectacular.

There is nothing to stop you from preparing a delightful meal and having a great Dinner, Lunch, or Midnight Snack – A LA TEXAS!

JANE EGGER

V

TABLE OF CONTENTS

INTRODUCTION

A LA - TEXAS is one of a series of efforts by Crabtree Publishing to collect prize recipes from the finest restaurants and bring them into your home and to your table. The collection is multi-ethnic and wide ranging including appetizers, salads, dressings, soups, sorbets, myriad entrees and many desserts. The cup runneth over with selections like Texas-Steak Salad, Strawberries Romanoff, Terrine of Salmon, Venison Stew and Cranberry Sorbet.

To acknowledge the purveyors of these palatable pleasures, we open their doors, sketch the varied decors, profile key personnel and set tables before you bearing delights from their kitchens.

In addition to our focus on fine food, we discuss Texas' booming wine industry. While Texas and wine may seem an anomaly to some, European blue-blood grapes are thriving in Texas soil and their wines are being stocked in stores and restaurants throughout the state. Our brief look into the past, present and future of the Texas wine industry concludes with a listing of several wineries and vineyards. Their proximity to some of Texas' more centrally located cities may encourage residents and tourists to leave town for the day and enjoy the Texas countryside while learning more of grapes and wine.

Our conclusion assumes the palate's needs were served and seeks to entice the reader to sample some of Texas' natural and social history and increased cultural leanings. The missions of San Antonio, Big Bend National Park, The Hill Country, San Jacinto and the state's various museums and galleries are all recognized for their ability to stir visceral juices and win the loyalties of campers, hikers, birdwatchers, painters, photographers, amateur historians, archeologists and those of us who just feel the need to move beyond sports complexes, movie theatres and amusement parks.

A LA - TEXAS is the first statewide effort by Crabtree Publishing.

— Continued —

While the territory required many investigative resources, Texas' unique self-perception required our treating the whole as well as our capacities would allow. Unlike some states that espouse a particular city or region, Texans tout Texas. To fractionalize Texas would scar the grain of the Live Oak and all that her roots encompass.

We visited several lovely restaurants who wished to partake but which we felt should be excluded from this particular venture. Our decision was based on their specialized menus and focus. If we organized another book on Texas Tearooms, "The Lagniappe" in Amarillo with its variety of compotes, sandwiches, soups, coffees and teas, would be in the forefront. In Fort Worth, "The Buffet" is located in a light and airy wing of the Kimball Art Museum and is a lovely spot for homemade soups, breads, desserts and cheese. These locations are a story unto themselves and deserve their own anthology.

The above mentioned adornments and qualifications behind, A La Texas bread and butter is food. Amidst the cornucopia to follow, there is a bit of Creole and Cajun nurtured along the Texas-Louisiana border, near the Sabine, in Mauriceville and Port Neches. Its marketability carried it further west, across the plains, to as unlikely a location as San Antonio where Creole Gumbo, Crayfish Bisque and Red Snapper Louisiane bolster the menu of a least one outstanding restaurant.

Hundreds of French affiliated enterprises in Dallas explain that city's array of first-class Gallic restaurants. Coupled with her emphasis on art, banking, international commerce and European styled hotels, it should be increasingly apparent why truffles, Bordeaux and sophisticated sauces are being deftly prepared and poured in many Dallas locations from small owner-chef enterprises to the grandest hostelries.

Houston, self-proclaimed our nation's number-one seaport in the handling of foreign tonnage, has a cultural diversity that spans the world, a fact clearly evidenced by the ninety

— Continued —

different languages spoken within her environs. While this ethnic potpourri engenders almost everything from Bavarian pastries to Zabaglione, the largest concentration of Asiatics in Texas is situated in and around Houston. Not surprisingly, Asian restaurants are sprinkled about as generously as soy sauce with Chinese and Japanese establishments the more visible.

Besides being the first Texas city to come into its own, some say San Antonio is the soul of Texas cooking. It is true that the first notable cuisine served in Texas was probably served at San Antonio's Menger Hotel. Opened in 1859, San Antonio River Turtle and buffalo were favorites on the menu. Yet, immigrants of the Canary Islands, a Spanish territory located off Africa's Northwest coast, were San Antonio's first permanent outside settlers.

Steaks, prime rib, chops and veal are well documented on Texas menus. However, Galveston Bay and the Gulf of Mexico also have made their presence known. Fish and shellfish have been swept well beyond Texan gulf shores and onto platters, plates and soup spoons from Beaumont to Amarillo. Wild game farms have also provided added bite and dimension to the state's menus. If this seems insufficient, modern transportation ensures a regular supply of Live Maine Lobster, Fresh Pacific Salmon, Venison from New Zealand and fresh fish available within twenty-four hours of their harvest from European waters.

Before you embark upon the following restaurants and culinary delights, let us say our efforts sought to maximize your success, minimize your frustration and entertain. All recipes have been properly tested and modifications made only where appropriate. Past efforts have refined our techniques and better apprised us of your wants and needs. However, for us to continue these endeavors, it is necessary you find A LA - TEXAS a reliable reference - a book deserving of gradual reduction to dog-ears, stains and personal notations. To this end we pray!

Vanilla in the corner
Yolk at the seam
Such organic endorsements
Make a publisher beam.

X

ANAQUA RESTAURANT

Four Seasons Hotel

The Anaqua Restaurant has the good fortune of being situated within the purview of the San Antonio Four Seasons Hotel. Located in the downtown area, this Four Seasons Hotel provides European-styled amenities that include 24-hour room service, a concierge, complimentary shoe shines, morning paper, limousine service and even bathrobes. The 250 balconized sleeping rooms overlook a large and small heated pool, tennis courts, health facilities and restored nineteenth century German dwellings that house pub facilities, private dining areas and conference rooms.

— Continued —

Unlike the large Anaqua tree that thrives within close proximity, the Anaqua Restaurant is in full bloom 12 months a year. This perpetual flowering is largely due to the exhaustive efforts of Executive Chef Joseph D. Cochran, Jr. In addition to hiring, training and directing a staff of several dozen, Chef Cochran is ultimately responsible for all the food that leaves the kitchen, whether it be eggs in the morning, a steak at dinner or a cheeseburger in the early morning hours. The chef's additional responsibilities of preparing for large receptions, poolside parties and his very popular weekly cooking class would seem to sap the energies of most men. However, his productivity shows no signs of turning fallow. Consistent quality, dilligent preparation and creative menus seem the order of the day, every day.

The Anaqua Restaurant has thrown the spotlight on great American cooking, believing that American cuisine and American chefs should take a backseat to no one. Portions are uniformly large and everything is fresh. Prior to ordering, one diner questioned whether the very popular Coho was fresh or fresh-frozen. Within minutes, he was staring down a clear-eyed, radiantly colored Coho, an obvious recent arrival from the Pacific Northwest.

The dinner menu's various salads and appetizers are novel and enticing. I selected the Hot Spinach Salad and thought it the most delicious salad course I had while venturing west of the Sabine. The bountiful portion of blanched greens was topped with a warm vinaigrette dressing that included red onion, bacon, mushrooms, diced scallions and tomatoes. Parmesan cheese capped the entire affair.

A heart swatch of America was revealed in a soup selection that included "Gooey Duck" Clam Stew, Southern Corn Chowder and Chicken Dumpling.

Main courses included a variety of fish, steaks, lamb, pasta, chicken, a uniquely prepared duck and a sentimental favorite of Chef Cochran's, the Veal Chop. This Texas-sized offering is served on a corn bread case that salutes this talented chef's

— Continued —

West Virginia origins. A generous portion of tender veal, oysters, huge chanterelle mushrooms, broccoli, asparagus and papaya all made for a truly delicious entree and evidence the Anaqua Restaurant's efforts to please.

Fruit pies, flans, pumpkin cheesecakes and homemade ice creams showed ample attempt to accommodate all the sweet toothed.

In keeping with the focus of its cuisine, the Anaqua Restaurant gives American wines center stage. The large selection is updated regularly by the hotel's Food and Beverage Director. A smooth 1981 ,Mount Eden Chardonnay guided me through my evening meal. Its sustained buttery taste, texture and bouquet left only positive impressions, no acidic residues.

For all those treading its inviting threshold, the Anaqua Restaurant should prove most enjoyable. The maitre d' and his staff provide a degree of attentiveness and courtesy that finds only commendation from this quarter. The casual elegance that both decor and staff work to convey is reinforced by floor-to-ceiling views of active Spanish fountains, well-tended gardens and strolling peacocks.

The Anaqua Restaurant is located at 555 S. Alamo in San Antonio.

VEAL CHOPS WITH MUSHROOM STUFFING

A LA - Anaqua Restaurant

¼	lb mushrooms (quartered)
2	cloves garlic (minced)
½	red onion (finely chopped)
½	celery stalk (finely chopped)
1	tomato (finely chopped)
¼	lb. butter (melted)
4	cups cornbread crumbs
	salt and pepper (to taste) *
1	pt. beef stock (you may substitute diluted canned consomme)
3	T. butter
¼	lb. mushrooms (quartered)
4	7 oz. veal chops
	salt and pepper (to season chops)
⅛	cup oil

1. Preheat oven to 350°.
2. Combine mushrooms, garlic, onion, celery and tomato. Saute in butter until onion is limp. Add cornbread crumbs and seasonings to taste. Heat well and set aside. Keep warm.
3. Cook stock until reduced in half; whisk in butter and add mushrooms. Keep warm.
4. Season chops. Brown in hot oil on both sides. Roast in oven 10 minutes for medium rare.
5. To serve, arrange dressing and chops on plates and pour sauce over chops.

— Continued —

Serves: 4
Preparation: 30 minutes

* Test kitchen also used sage, fines herbs and fresh chopped parsley to taste.

Chef suggests serving with canned peach half and steamed broccoli. This is an excellent combination!

ROAST DUCK WITH NECTARINES
(Begin early in day or day before)

A LA - Anaqua Restaurant

1	**whole duck**
1	**carrot (sliced)**
1	**stalk celery (sliced)**
½	**medium onion (chopped)**
1	**bay leaf**
1	**gal. water**
	rosemary (to taste)
	thyme (to taste)
	salt and pepper (to taste)
¼	**cup sugar**
2	**cups water**
	fresh nectarine (or canned or frozen)
1	**T. sugar**
¼	**cup nectarine liqueur or brandy**
3	**T. butter (softened)**

1. Separate legs and thighs from body of the duck. Remove meat from bone and trim off all excess fat.
2. Remove wing tips and neck bone.
3. Brown all the removed bones in frying pan. Pour off excess grease. (This can be saved. It is excellent to cook with.)
4. In a stock pot, put browned bones, carrot, celery, onion, bay leaf and water. Simmer until reduced to 1 quart of liquid. Strain liquid; discard bones and vegetables.
5. In frying pan, sear **leg** and **thigh** meat over medium-high heat. Drain off all excess grease.
6. Add browned meat to stock and cook until duck is tender and stock has been reduced by half again, approximately thirty minutes.
7. Preheat oven to 350°.

— Continued —

8. Season cavity and outside of duck with rosemary, thyme, salt and pepper. Sear in hot pan. Finish cooking in 350° oven to medium rare. (Approximately 15 min. for a 4 lb. duck).

9. Remove from oven. Remove skin from duck breast. Julienne* skin and fry until very crisp. Pour off grease. Save skin.

10. Remove meat from bone; slice thinly; keep warm.

11. Combine sugar and water in saucepan. Bring to a boil. Poach nectarine until skin easily slips off. Cut in half; remove seed. Slice each half into three slices.

12. Remove leg and thigh meat from stock. Keep warm.

13. Add 1 T. sugar, nectarine liqueur or brandy. Heat. Fold in butter until well incorporated.

14. To serve, arrange some leg and thigh meat on plate. Top with breast slices arranged in fan shape. Arrange nectarine slices over meat. Garnish with crisp skin. Pour sauce over top.

Serves: 2
Preparation: 3 hours

* See Glossary.

Test kitchen recommends doing recipe in two stages. Prepare up through step six ahead of time. Finish final preparations an hour or so before serving.

The Anaqua Restaurant accompanies the duck with steamed asparagus spears.

HOT SPINACH SALAD

A LA - Anaqua Restaurant

½   lb. bacon (diced into 1" X ½" pieces)
½   red onion (thinly sliced)
½   lb. mushrooms (quartered)
⅓   cup vinegar *
½   cup chicken stock
1   lb. fresh spinach
     salt and pepper (to taste)
¼ - ⅓ cup grated Parmesan cheese

1.   Saute bacon until three-quarters brown; pour off one half bacon fat and add onions and mushrooms; saute.
2.   Add vinegar and stock. Heat.
3.   Drop in spinach and toss until just wilted. Leaves should be crisp. Add salt and pepper to taste.
4.   Serve immediately by arranging on individual plates. Sprinkle with Parmesan.

Serves: 2 as main course
        4 as a side dish
Preparation: 15 minutes

* Chef recommends: champagne or tarragon vinegar.

Always try to grate your own Parmesan as it is much tastier than the canned variety.

Easy and delicious!

8

Austin's Courtyard

If one's interests lie in quality food, regally prepared and served within the likeness of a European dwelling, Austin's Courtyard is the place to gather.

Located in Austin, just north of the Colorado River on Lamar, its European-styled cuisine, Epicurean dinners and decor create an atmosphere that is at variance with much of the competition.

Interior masonry walls support sloping eaves of Spanish tile, antiqued windows and dark wooden doors and moldings. These same walls skirt an inner courtyard complete with tables. The shadowy interior's amber lighting sheds a torch-like quality upon rough beige walls and tiles, creating a scene suitable for swordplay a la Errol Flynn and Captain Blood. Sounds of Spanish guitars would seem most appropriate, but on the evening of my visit, a piano rendition of "Autumn Leaves" was no less enjoyed.

I was escorted past the full-service bar area and seated in a smaller dining room that was similarly clad in beige stucco,

— Continued —

dark woods and carpeting.

The table setting was quite impressive. Crisp gray on white linen undercut a hurricane lamp housing a flickering white candle. The china, white with silver rim, was complemented by a narrow vase housing small red carnations and leather fern.

Chef Gert Rausch and Horst Pfeifer author not only a very creative and everchanging menu, but one presented on rolled parchment and bound in maroon ribbon.

Eight or nine appetizers included California Goat Cheese on Limestone Lettuce, Louisiana Crayfish Salad, Belgium Smoked Salmon and Salade ala Maison with Blue Cheese Dressing. I had the latter and have to say it bore no sign of afterthought. A good-sized plate was worked to its limit with a pyramid of dark green Boston leaf lettuce, healthy sections of tomato, watercress, green pepper and cucumber.

Approximately fifteen entrees included the popular Hill Country Quail with Chanterelles, Roasted Goose Breast Provencale, Carpetbagger Steak, Sweetbreads, Gulf Grouper in Papillote and my selection, Louisiana Redfish. The delicate fresh fish was covered with what appeared to be a Marsala sauce and flanked with broccoli flowerettes resting atop a baked tomato and a lightly toasted mashed potato croquette.

If your demands are more regal in nature, a twenty-four hour notice affords you the choice of seven Epicurean Dinners. A Roasted Lamb Loin is baked in light pastry and served with a bouquetiere of legumes. A Scottish Pheasant is stuffed, roasted and served with wild rice, candied fruit and a sauce of peach liqueur.

Approximately eight dessert items range from the delicious Sacher Torte to Coffee Pierre flamed tableside. Other choices include Banana Flambee, Cheesecake with Kiwi and Strawberries in Cream.

Austin's Courtyard offers the Courtyard - or main dining room - smaller rooms with darkened corners and quieter seating, and the larger private dining rooms for group gatherings. But,

— Continued —

wherever your table, a European flavor shares your quarters with subtleties of simmering soups, tender fowl baking under the sweet persuasiveness of a brandy sauce and a general mood of contentment among the patrons.

Austin's Courtyard is located at 1205 N. Lamar in Austin.

LOUISIANA REDFISH FILLED WITH SCALLOP MOUSSE
(Begin at least 45 minutes in advance)

A LA - AUSTIN'S COURTYARD

— Mousse —

¼	lb. fresh scallops
	salt and freshly ground pepper (to taste)
1	egg
3	T. whipping cream
4	redfish fillets, 1 lb. each, or any fish fillet of choice
1	T. butter
2	T. shallots (minced)
1	cup dry white wine
¾	cup whipping cream
1	t. ginger (ground)
	fresh dill for garnish
16	cooked asparagus spears (garnish)

— Mousse —

1. Combine scallops, salt and pepper in food processor. Puree about 30 seconds.
2. Add egg and mix 30 seconds. Transfer to bowl and refrigerate 30 minutes.
3. Remove from refrigerator and beat in cream in slow steady stream until well blended.

4. With sharp knife cut a pocket in top of each fillet. Fill with scallop mousse.
5. Spread butter over bottom of large skillet. Sprinkle with shallots.
6. Arrange fillets in skillet; add wine; season with salt and pepper.

— Continued —

7. Cover skillet; place over high heat. Bring wine to boil; reduce heat and simmer four minutes. Shake pan gently to prevent sticking.
8. Remove cover; add cream and ginger.
9. Over medium heat, cook sauce until thickened and reduced to one cup. Adjust seasonings.
10. Remove fish to warm platter. Spoon sauce over fish. Garnish with dill and asparagus spears. Serve immediately.

Serves: 4
Preparation: 30 minutes

This is a divine dish. The flavors are wonderful!

SACHER TORTE COURTYARD

A LA - AUSTIN'S COURTYARD

2	oz. unsweetened chocolate
½	cup unsalted butter
1	cup water
½	cup buttermilk
2	cups flour (sifted)
2	cups sugar
1½	t. baking soda
2	eggs
½	t. vanilla
2	cups apricot preserves
2	T. Grand Marnier liqueur
½	cup Grand Marnier
2	oz. unsweetened chocolate
¼	cup water
2	cups powdered sugar
1	T. Grand Marnier
1	cup whipped cream

1. Preheat oven to 375°.
2. Grease and flour two 9" cake pans.
3. In top of double boiler combine 2 ounces chocolate, butter and one cup water. Heat until chocolate melts.
4. Add buttermilk; stir until blended.
5. Stir in flour. Add sugar, baking soda, eggs and vanilla. Mix well.
6. Pour into cake pans. Bake for 40 minutes.
7. Cool 10 minutes in pans. Remove from pans and cool completely.
8. Split each layer in half so that you have four layers.
9. To make filling, combine apricot preserves with 2 T. Grand Marnier. Set aside.

— Continued —

10. Next, brush each layer with Grand Marnier, using ½ cup total. Then spread 3 layers with apricot preserves mixture and stack on top of each other. Top layer will have only Grand Marnier.
11. Make a glaze by melting 2 ounces unsweetened chocolate with ¼ cup water. Add powdered sugar and 1 T. Grand Marnier.
12. Pour glaze over cake and smooth top and sides with spatula dipped in hot water.
13. Refrigerate until ready to serve.
14. Top with whipped cream and serve.

Serves: 10
Preparation: 30 minutes
Bake: 40 minutes

A wonderfully rich chocolate cake for any festive occasion!

HILL COUNTRY QUAIL* WITH SHALLOTS AND SAUCE JURASIENNE

A LA - AUSTIN'S COURTYARD

16	large shallots (peeled)
2	T. oil
	salt and freshly ground pepper
8	quails or 4 Cornish game hens (halved) *
1½	t. raspberry vinegar
1½	cups veal stock or chicken broth
6	peppercorns
1	t. garlic (chopped)
2	T. unsalted butter
	watercress for garnish

1. Preheat oven to 475°. Place shallots in oven proof pan. Sprinkle with oil and season with salt and pepper.
2. Bake shallots until soft, about twenty minutes.
3. Pat quails dry and season with salt and pepper, inside and out.
4. Stuff quails with two shallots each. Heat remaining oil from shallots in pan over medium heat. Arrange quails in pan, breast side down and brown lightly.
5. Turn quails over. Place pan in oven. Roast 6 - 7 minutes for rare or until done to your liking. (Frozen Cornish Hens take about 20 - 30 minutes). Transfer quails to warm platter.
6. Remove grease from pan. Place pan over medium heat; add vinegar and stir.
7. Add stock, peppercorns and garlic. Cook until sauce has thickened and is reduced by half.
8. Remove from heat and whisk in butter, one tablespoon at a time. Spoon sauce over quails; garnish with watercress.

Serves: 8
Preparation: 45 minutes

* This dish is equally good with Cornish hens.

Sauce is superb!

16

Located in northern Dallas' rose-hued, granite girdled Westin Hotel, Blom's took little time in establishing itself as one of Dallas' very finest dining rooms. The most elaborate of the hotel's three restaurants, Blom's decor is not overdone; comfortable, classic furnishings include wing-back chairs, love seats and banquettes. Table settings of fresh flowers, candles, sterling silver and white china of simple sophistication merit inspection before chairs are drawn.

Accompanying the culinary accomplishments brought to your table, the staff, from the tuxedoed to those in white aprons, is truly professional.

Serving lunch, dinner and a weekend brunch, Blom's provides still further opportunity to display the staff's penchant for creativity and perfection by changing its menu on a regular basis.

Almost a dozen hot and cold appetizers include Raviolis of Salmon and Mushrooms, Trout Mousse wrapped in Smoked Salmon and a Char-Broiled Quail with Spinach and Fresh Herb Sauce.

Salads range from a unique Duck and Partridge with Pear-Vinaigrette Dressing to a Warm Goat Cheese Salad with Raspberry Dressing.

— Continued —

Entrees offer Texas Lamb as evidence in the Venison and Lamb Combination with Onion Puree and Poivrade Sauce. Steamed North Sea Turbot with a Light Parsley Sauce and Julienne of Carrots provides lighter fare and room for the popular desserts which include Pear-Butterscotch and Chocolate Marquise.

The weekend brunch offers four course entrees which utilize the egg in a variety of popular presentations and includes freshly squeezed fruit juice, fresh fruit plates and a choice of elaborate breakfast pastries.

Blom's seems determined to maintain the Westin Hotel's reputation for superior dining as well as quality lodging.

Blom's is located in the Westin Hotel at 13340 Dallas Parkway in Dallas.

ALMOND BRIE OMELETTE WITH GREEN PEPPERCORN SAUCE

A LA - Blom's

1	T. butter
1	T. shallots (chopped)
1	T. cognac
¼	cup red wine
½	cup beef stock or bouillon
½	cup whipping cream
3	T. butter
½	t. green peppercorns (avail. in gourmet or spice section)
	salt (to taste)
8	eggs
¼	lb. Brie (cut in thin slices)
½	oz. flaked almonds (garnish)

1. In a saucepan, melt butter. Add shallots; saute until limp.
2. Add cognac and flame*. Add red wine and cook over medium heat until reduced by half.
3. Pour in stock and reduce by half again. Put in cream and butter and reduce by half. Add green peppercorns and salt to taste. Keep warm over low heat.
4. Make four 2-egg omelettes. Place Brie in center of each before rolling.
5. To serve, pour sauce on 4 plates, top with individual omelettes. Garnish with almonds.

Serves: 4
Preparation: 1 hour (sauce)
minutes for omelettes

* If you're not familiar with this step, see Glossary under Flambe.

An unusual omelette for late night suppers or after theater parties. Easy!

SALAD OF DUCK AND PARTRIDGE WITH PEAR VINEGAR DRESSING

A LA - Blom's

1	duck breast (thinly sliced - cooked)
1	partridge or chicken breast (thinly sliced - cooked)
¼	cup olive oil

— Dressing —

⅓	cup pear vinegar or red wine vinegar
1	t. chervil
1	t. tarragon
1	T. lemon juice
	salt and pepper (to taste)
½	ripe pear (pureed)*
¼	cup olive oil
¼	cup salad oil

1	head radicchio or substitute red leaf lettuce (washed, lightly torn and chilled)
1	head endive (washed, lightly torn and chilled)
2	leaves escarole or romaine (washed, lightly torn and chilled)
	small bunch of red seedless grapes (washed and halved)

1. Marinate breast meats in olive oil for 10 - 20 minutes.

— Dressing —

2. Combine vinegar, chervil, tarragon, lemon juice, salt and pepper (to taste) and pureed pear in food processor or blender. Process to combine ingredients.
3. With motor running, slowly add both oils. Adjust seasonings to taste with salt and pepper if necessary.

— Continued —

4. Combine radicchio, endive and escarole in medium size bowl. Mix with enough dressing to lightly coat salad ingredients.
5. Divide into 4 portions on salad plates.
6. Cook meats over medium high heat until just done, 4 - 5 minutes.
7. Place meat slices on top of salad.
8. Garnish with grapes and serve.

Serves: 4 as 1st course
Preparation: 30 minutes

*Peel, core and puree pear in blender or use canned pear and puree in blender.

Try this as an unusual beginning for a holiday meal. Use the vinaigrette on any green salad or fresh fruit salad.

VENISON* AND LAMB WITH ONION PUREE AND POIVRADE SAUCE(Marinate venison overnight)

A LA - Blom's

— Sauce —

	oil (to saute)
2	lbs. venison and lamb bones (or all lamb bones)
1	carrot (finely chopped)
1	onion (finely chopped)
1	leek, white only (finely chopped)
1	stalk celery (finely chopped)
	salt and pepper (to taste)
2	T. vinegar
1	cup burgundy wine
2	qts. beef stock (substitute diluted boullion if you wish)
¼	cup butter (softened)
¼	cup flour
½	cup red currant jelly
1	medium white onion (diced)
¼	cup whipping cream
	butter (to saute)
8	lamb chops (approximately 5 oz. each)
4	venison fillet mignons (4 oz. each) marinated overnight in burgundy wine
	or 4 lamb fillets from loin. (No need to marinate lamb.)*

— Sauce —

1. Brown bones in large stock pot in oil. Add carrot, onion, leek, celery and salt and pepper. Cook until vegetables are limp.
2. Add vinegar and cook until reduced to almost nothing.
3. Add wine and beef stock. Cook until reduced by half.
4. Strain and return sauce to saucepan. Reduce again by one third.

— Continued —

5. In a small bowl, combine butter and flour into smooth paste.
6. Add slowly to warm sauce and wisk until sauce is a velvety smooth consistency.
7. Add currant jelly and keep sauce warm.

8. Place diced onion in blender and blend until fine.
9. Cook onion puree in separate saucepan. Bring to slow simmer. Add cream and reduce by half. Set onion puree aside.
10. Preheat oven to 350°.
11. If using venison, drain from marinade. Season lamb and venison with salt and pepper.
12. Saute meat in butter over moderate heat until browned equally on both sides.
13. Transfer to oven and cook until medium, about 10-15 minutes.
14. Remove from oven.
15. To serve: coat plates with sauce and place 2 chops on each. Place a small mound of onion puree on each and top with venison mignon or lamb fillet. Pour additional sauce on top.

Serves: 4
Preparation: 2 hours
Marinate: Overnight (if using venison)

*If you are fortunate to have venison try it this way. Equally good with lamb.

A wonderful presentation!

PEAR BUTTERSCOTCH
(Begin several hours ahead)

A LA - Blom's

4	pears
1	cup granulated sugar
2	pints water
¼	cup butter
½	cup firmly packed brown sugar
1	T. water
½	cup plus 1 T. half and half
4	scoops vanilla ice cream
4	rosettes whipping cream (garnish)
4	mint leaves (garnish)

1. Peel pears with a small knife.
2. Combine sugar and water and heat. Gently poach pears in syrup until just tender, approximately five minutes.
3. Allow pears to cool in syrup.
4. When cool, remove core from pears and chill pears.
5. Melt butter in heavy saucepan. Add sugar and cook slowly for one minute.
6. Add water and bring to a boil.
7. Add cream slowly, stirring. Simmer gently for five minutes. Strain. Sauce may be served hot or cold.
8. To serve, coat bottom of dessert dish with butterscotch sauce.
9. Slice off small part at base of pear and stand upright on top of sauce. Place one scoop of ice cream beside pear. Garnish with whipped cream and mint leaf.

Serves: 4
Preparation: 20 minutes

A rich dessert. A sure hit with guests!

CAFÉ ANNIE

Styled after the elegant cafes and bistros of Europe, New York and San Francisco, and imbued with American spirit, Cafe Annie offers a warm, understated atmosphere with excellent service and exceptional cuisine.

The restaurant provides an alternative to the highly formal establishments of Houston and the proliferation of hamburger and steakhouse operations. Wood panelled walls, brass railings and etched glass create a warm and relaxed feeling, while the service staff provide a sense of festivity and excitement.

Robert Del Grande is Executive Chef and Partner at Cafe Annie. Del Grande, who holds a Ph.D. in Biochemistry, has earned a reputation as one of the finest and most innovative chefs in the country. His menus have taken Cafe Annie to the forefront of cuisine in Houston. Based on fine fresh ingredients from local suppliers as well as international purveyors, Cafe Annie's cuisine reflects a strong European heritage updated with American exuberance and style. Although the menu changes with the seasons, entrees always include fine veal, lamb, chicken, beef and fish. Game dishes have become the restaurant's specialty.

— Continued —

Mimi Del Grande, the chef's wife, manages the restaurant. Her personal touches in the dining room, her warm reception at the front door and her constant attention to the needs of the customers give Cafe Annie a bright sparkle. "My goal is to create a mood of warmth and comfort," says Mimi. "I treat the restaurant like my home. Every day is like a dinner party, with fresh flowers and a wonderful mix of interesting people."

Finally, with an extensive wine list that evidences much thought and consultation, it should come as no surprise that Cafe Annie was featured on the cover of a popular national magazine as one of the country's fine restaurants.

Cafe Annie is located at 5858 Westheimer in Houston.

CHOCOLATE PECAN TORTE

A LA - Cafe Annie

1	pie crust (unbaked)
2	T. butter
3	oz. unsweetened chocolate
¾	cup sugar
½	t. salt
2	T. flour
1	cup dark syrup
3	eggs
1½	t. vanilla
1¾	cups pecans

1. Preheat oven to 350°.
2. Melt butter and chocolate together in double boiler and set aside.
3. Meanwhile, mix sugar, salt and flour in separate bowl.
4. Stir in syrup and eggs.
5. Add melted butter and chocolate.
6. Add vanilla and pecans and blend all ingredients.
7. Pour into unbaked pie crust using an 11" quiche pan with removable bottom. *
8. Bake 1 hour or until firm to the touch. Cool and serve.

Preparation: 15 minutes
Baking time: 1 hour

* The torte pan is optional, but it makes it easier to serve.

Very good, very rich and very easy!

BREAST OF CHICKEN WITH POACHED PEAR

A LA - Cafe Annie

4	chicken breasts (boneless)
4	pears *
1	cup water
1	cup white wine
2	T. sugar
1	T. lemon juice
1	cup chicken stock
2	T. shallots (diced)
½	cup heavy cream
2	T. butter (to saute chicken)
¼	cup butter

1. Preheat oven to 350°.
2. Peel pears. slice in half, remove cores, and poach until tender in water, wine, sugar and lemon juice.
3. Remove pears and allow to cool. Save poaching liquid.
4. Puree 2 of the pears in a blender. Set aside.
5. Cook pear poaching liquid over high heat until reduced by half. Add chicken stock and shallots and reduce by half again.
6. Next, add pear puree and cream; cook over low heat and stir until slightly thickened. Do not boil.
7. While sauce is cooking, melt 2 T. butter in a large frying pan. Quickly saute chicken breasts on both sides until brown.
8. Place breasts in oven at 350° for 6 minutes or until done. Keep hot.
9. Meanwhile, break up ¼ cup butter into small nuggets and whisk, one at a time, into sauce.

— Continued —

10. Slice the 4 pear halves across the axis and fan the slices onto 4 dinner plates. Slice the chicken breasts and fan these slices next to the pear. Cover with sauce and serve.

Serves: 4
Preparation: 35 minutes

*If good fresh ones aren't available, use canned pears.

Elegant looking and tasting!

J. SNITILY 86 ©

Café Royal
Plaza of the Americas Hotel

The Cafe Royal, modeled after the famed Cafe Royal in London, is a very impressive restaurant set in an equally impressive hotel. Located in downtown Dallas, the Plaza of the Americas Hotel deserves the close inspection even of passers-by. The 442 room hotel, the sheltered multi-level parking facility and twin commercial buildings at either end enclose an expansive atrium that houses a large skating rink surrounded by retail shops, restaurants and cafes. Offering all the elegance of a fine European hotel, Plaza of the Americas also features a health club, foreign currency exchange, afternoon tea and, of course, excellent cuisine.

The Cafe Royal was located behind white double doors that portended something special. My expectations were fulfilled. The Cafe Royal was one of the most handsome dining rooms I've had the pleasure of entering. Burgundy carpeting with small floral patterns, walls of tasteful fabric, richly upholstered banquettes, European oils in elegant gilt frames, beautiful porcelain vases and lamps, leather upholstered arm chairs, tear-dropped chandeliers, Galway crystal, Wedgewood china and International silver, all provided a setting yet to fade from memory.

— Continued —

The waiters, some bearing European accents, were truly professional men, not boys – alert, diligent and most gracious even to a party of one. To find another staff by whom they were upstaged would be difficult.

Dining at the noon hour, I found the luncheon selections superb, and from this writer's perspective, reflected a well coordinated effort to see that the cuisine – as is often the case – was not outdone by decor. Specifically, rather than offering the standard opening of sliced French bread, the Cafe Royal had soft, warm, glazed rolls that were simply the tastiest rolls I had in Texas. An excellent pureed zucchini cream soup, served very hot, retained its individuality rather than being merely the requisite bridge to an entree.

The entrees were varied, including beef, fish and fowl. I selected an excellent monkfish, served upon julienned endive and topped with a patiently prepared Red Bell Pepper Sauce.

I was surprised by the thoughtfully prepared side dishes that accompanied my entree. Snow peas, neither overcooked nor too crisp, potato fritters that bore no oily residues, and zucchini with red peppers and onions formed an unexpected and very delicious triad.

As with the soup, the coffee suffered no evidence of afterthought. Borne on a silver service, its quality wrote its own self supporting chapter in what I found to be a novel dining experience.

Desserts included souffles and a most impressive dessert cart which bore a solid black and white chocolate mousse. Caramel custard, unassuming as it is, will often test a restaurant's adherence to quality control. I neither saw nor ingested any transgressions from uniform excellence.

The Cafe Royal's receipt of the "Cartier Elegance in Dining Award", the "Wedgewood Award" and five stars, are from my experience, totally justified.

Cafe Royal is located at 650 N. Pearl St. in Dallas.

LES ESCARGOTS DE BOURGOGNE AU CHABLIS
Vineyard Snails with Chablis, Grapes and Walnuts
in Herb Butter

A LA - Cafe Royal

– Herb Butter –

¾   cup butter (softened)
6   T. parsley (chopped)
6   T. chives (chopped)
3   T. "fines herbs" (purchase in grocery spice section)

32   snails (out of shell)
¼   cup butter
½   cup Chablis wine
¼   cup walnuts (coarsely chopped)
24   white grapes (peeled)
4   puff pillows or patty shells (baked)*
4   lemon leaves or other small green leaf for garnish

1. Combine softened butter, parsley, chives and herbs. Mix well. Set aside.
2. Melt butter in pan; saute snails.
3. Add Chablis and cook until reduced by half.
4. Add walnuts and grapes.
5. Whisk in herb butter, little by little.
6. To serve, cut puff pillow in half, or remove top of patty shell. Place snails in center and pour sauce over and around. Cover with top and garnish with leaf.

Serves: 4
Preparation: 30 minutes

* See frozen food section of your grocery. If you use Patty Shells you may need to use a couple for each person, depending on their size.

A great combination of flavors. Snail lovers will be ecstatic!

LA SOUP DE HOMARD AU BASILIC
Fresh Lobster Soup with Basil

A LA - Cafe Royal

1	medium lobster (approximately 2½ lbs.) or 2 medium tails in the shells
1	T. olive oil
½	cup combined leeks, carrots and celery (chopped)
1	T. brandy
1	qt. fish stock * or canned clam juice
½	cup fresh tomatoes (cubed)
1	t. garlic
1	t. fresh basil or ½ t. dry
1	t. fresh tarragon or ½ t. dry
1	T. lobster butter (combine ½ T. fresh butter with ½ T. ground lobster meat
	fresh basil leaves for garnish
8	garlic toast rounds

1. Cut lobster into pieces. Saute in hot olive oil.
2. Add chopped vegetables, cook for 4 minutes.
3. Add brandy. Allow to warm then ignite with match and flambe.
4. Add fish stock, tomato, garlic, basil and tarragon. Simmer 5 minutes.
5. Remove lobster meat from shells. Put meat into soup.
6. Add lobster butter and stir to thicken slightly.
7. Serve in individual bowls garnished with basil. Serve with garlic toast rounds.

— Continued —

_____

* Test kitchen made a fish stock out of:

2	**lbs. fresh snapper**
2	**bay leaves**
¼	**cup carrot (chopped)**
¼	**cup celery (chopped)**
¼	**cup onion (chopped)**
1	**qt. water**

Simmer ingredients for 10 - 15 minutes and strain stock. Quick method: use canned clam juice.

Serves: 4
Preparation: 15 minutes

The flavor combinations are outstanding!

SMOKED SALMON SOUFFLE

A LA - Cafe Royal

4   **(5") souffle dishes (buttered)**

– Savory Souffle Base Mix –

2   **cups milk**
2   **T. butter**
5   **egg yolks**
3   **whole eggs**
5   **T. flour**
      salt, pepper, nutmeg (to taste)
3   **oz. Gruyere cheese (grated) ***

2   **oz. smoked salmon (flaked)**
1   **oz. avocado (chopped)**
2   **t. chives (chopped)**
8   **egg whites**

– Savory Souffle Base Mix –

1. Bring milk and butter to boil.
2. Add yolks, whole eggs, flour and seasonings. Cook until thick. Taste to make sure raw taste of flour is gone.
3. Let cool. Add cheese. This is your base mix.

4. Meanwhile, mix together salmon, avocado and chives, and stir into base mix.
5. Beat egg whites until stiff; carefully fold into base mix.
6. Fill your buttered souffle dishes to rim.
7. Hit dishes a few times on table to release air bubbles.
8. Bake at 350° for 10-15 minutes until set. Set dishes into "artichoke folded" cloth napkins and serve immediately.

— Continued —

SMOKED SALMON SOUFFLE — Continued

Serves: 4
Preparation: 35 minutes
Baking time: 10 (plus) minutes

* Or your choice of similar cheese.

L'ESCALOPE DE TURBOT AUX FRAMBOISE

Sauteed Turbot Escalope with Raspberry Sauce

A LA - Cafe Royal

2	cups raspberries or 2 cups frozen without syrup
1	cup shallots (chopped)
2	T. raspberry vinegar
2	cups fish stock or canned clam juice
1	cup butter (cut into small pieces)
4	6 oz. turbot fillets, seasoned with flour, salt and pepper
4	oz. clarified butter *
1	cup sliced chantrelle mushrooms or other mushrooms (sauteed)
¼	cup chives (finely chopped)

1. In saucepan, cook raspberries and shallots until all juice evaporates. Do not brown shallots.
2. Add raspberry vinegar, stirring up any particles.
3. Add fish stock and reduce to ⅓ by cooking.
4. Bit by bit, whisk in small pieces of butter. Keep heat low.
5. Strain sauce through a fine sieve. Keep warm.
6. Saute fillets in clarified butter for 5 minutes or until fillets are done.
7. To serve, place sauce in center of plate, top with fish fillet and garnish with mushrooms and chives.

Serves: 4
Preparation: 20 minutes

* See Glossary.

An interesting, sweet tart combination. I found it refreshing.

CALLUAUD

Guy and Martine Calluaud have spent thousands of kitchen hours in locales as diverse as Morocco, Nice, New York and now Dallas, before opening Calluaud.

Guy's family has long been associated with famous chefs and fine dining. His great-grandmother was chef to Napoleon III and his father, Pierre, possesses cooking skills long respected in both Morocco and France.

Guy acquired his skills at an early age by working in his father's kitchen learning many facets of traditional French cooking.

After their marriage, Guy and Martine both worked in the popular Calluaud family restaurant. In time, however, they decided to strike out on their own and move to the United States.

As Guy's cooking began drawing larger and larger audiences, Martine kept pace by locating, financing and opening progressively larger and more sophisticated settings in which Guy could display his talents.

Calluaud is the couple's latest showcase for Guy's broadly-based cooking skills and Martine's sound business judgment. This multi-star French restaurant is an elegant domain with walls of beige-colored fabric and tables topped with fresh roses.

— Continued —

Each menu selection, whether it be an appetizer, entree or dessert, is a masterpiece in terms of both artistry and taste.

Appetizers include the popular Galantine Volaille - a chicken pate in champagne aspic with pistachio nuts. Entree selections may consist of Breast of Chicken, Pike Quenelles with Shrimp or Veal Sweetbreads. Because Guy is also a licensed patissier, desserts are no less visually and literally savored.

Calluaud is located at 2619 McKinney in Dallas.

SAUMON FRAIS AU SABAYON DE CAVIAR
Fresh Salmon with Caviar Sabayon

A LA - Calluaud

4	8 oz. filets of salmon
¼	cup dry white wine
2	t. shallots (chopped)
2	t. unsalted butter
4	egg yolks
½	lime (juiced)
¼	cup whipping cream
4	t. black American caviar
	white pepper (to taste)
	salt (to taste)

1. Combine salmon, wine, shallots and butter in skillet. Place skillet over high heat and bring wine to boil. Cover skillet; lower heat; cook for 1 minute. Turn off heat and let sit for 6 minutes.
2. Remove salmon to serving dish and keep warm. Reserve cooking liquid.
3. Place egg yolks in stainless top of double boiler. Add lime juice and beat until well mixed.
4. Add remaining ingredients, including cooking liquid. Stir well and place over hot water in double boiler.
5. Heat until mixture thickens to consistency of rich gravy. Taste for seasonings. Add white pepper and salt if you desire.
6. Pour over salmon and serve.

Serves: 4
Preparation: 20 minutes

A delicious flavor combination.
The caviar sauce would be delicious over any white fish.

BREAST OF PHEASANT

A LA - Calluaud

1	whole pheasant breast or whole chicken breast
¼	t. freshly grated ginger root
	salt and pepper (to taste)
½	T. butter
½	t. chopped onion
3	juniper berries * (optional)
½	head of endive or heart of chicory (cut Julienne) **
1	small carrot, cut into 6-8 sticks
1	T. very dry sherry
2	T. chicken stock
1	T. butter

1. One hour before cooking, spread ginger over breast. Set aside.
2. Salt and pepper breast.
3. Melt ½ tablespoon butter in medium skillet over high heat.
4. Put breast in skillet; lightly brown on both sides, approximately 5 minutes. Remove to dish and keep warm.
5. In same skillet saute onion. Add berries, endive and carrots. Stir to mix.
6. Place breast of pheasant on vegetable mixture in skillet. Add sherry and stock. Cover and cook for 6 - 8 minutes over medium low temperature until breast is cooked.
7. Remove breast. Remove vegetables with slotted spoon and place on serving plate.
8. Slice breast in thin pieces and arrange on top of vegetables.
9. Pour any juices back into pan. Place over high heat and reduce by half.
10. Lower flame and add remaining tablespoon of butter, stirring until butter is melted.

— Continued —

11. Taste for seasonings and add salt and pepper if necessary. Pour butter over breast. Serve immediately.

Serves: 2
Preparation time: 30 minutes
Marinate: 1 hour

 * Available in spice shops
**Julienne means to cut into 1½" long, very thin strips.

This is a wonderfully flavored dish! Very easy to fix!

RIS DE VEAU AU VIN DE SAUTERNE

Sweetbreads with Sauterne Wine

A LA - Calluaud

2	lbs. veal sweetbreads
¼	cup vinegar
2	T. butter (divided)
¼	cup flour
	salt and pepper
1	medium onion (finely chopped)
40	white grapes (blanched and peeled)
4	oz. sauterne wine
2	T. unsalted butter

1. Soak sweetbreads in large quantity of cold water for one hour. Drain.
2. Boil 3 quarts salted water. Add sweetbreads and vinegar. Cook 10 minutes.
3. Immediately remove from heat and place in cold water until cool.
4. Remove membranes, vessels and cartilage.
5. Melt 1 T. butter in large pan over high heat.
6. Flour and salt and pepper sweetbreads and brown quickly on both sides.
7. Remove from pan. Add onions and brown.
8. Add grapes, sauterne and sweetbreads. Cover and cook 4 minutes on low.
9. Remove sweetbreads to serving platter. Keep warm.
10. To pan, add last tablespoon of butter; stir until melted.
11. Pour over sweetbreads. Serve immediately.

Serves: 4
Soak: 1 hour
Preparation: 30 minutes
Cooking: 15 minutes

Delicious combination!

CHEZ SUZETTE

Located in Lubbock's Quaker Square Shopping Center on the former site of La Scala Restaurant, Chez Suzette has merged the best of La Scala's menu with the best of another former dining spot, La Crepe Suzette. The result is French-Italian or what some might call Continental.

An informal, bistro-like interior makes effective use of the red, white and blue awnings that formerly hung outside La Crepe Suzette. Round and square tables are graced with either red or pink linen and petite gas lamps. Ceiling fans circle over an area swathed in soft light and subtle notes of French and Italian recordings. Former patrons of La Crepe Suzette may recognize the huge butcher's block that dominates the entry area as well as some smaller memorabilia.

The cooking is done on location by the owner-chef, who is a native of France, and several sous-chefs. In addition to the recipes which follow, other popular entrees include Pepper Steak, Snapper Puff Pastry and a Prima Vera that deftly incorporates linguine, ham, mushrooms, peas, cream and Parmesan.

Chez Suzette's dessert selection includes several items also available as take-outs from the pastry bar. Favorites include a Chocolate Truffle Mousse, assorted fresh napoleons and the very lightest crepes, wrapped around mounds of ice cream and topped with whipped cream and chocolate flakes.

A full service bar is well stocked with California, French and Italian wines, as well as imported and domestic beers. Cappuccino and espresso are also available and within minutes of your table. Appealing to all ages, professions and occupations, Chez Suzette is amply prepared to attend to your luncheon and dinner needs.

Chez Suzette is located at 4423 50th St., Quaker Square, in Lubbock.

LE VACHERIN
Glamorous Meringue, Strawberry and Ice Cream Dessert

A LA - Chez Suzette

1	large pastry bag for meringue
6	egg whites at room temperature
¼	t. salt
¼	t. cream of tartar
1	cup granulated sugar
2	t. vanilla extract
1	additional cup of sugar
2	baking sheets (buttered and floured)
14	large strawberries
1	t. strawberry liqueur
1	cup whipped cream
1	cup strawberry ice cream

1. Preheat oven to 250°.
2. Beat egg whites at slow speed until frothy. Add salt and cream of tartar.
3. Continue beating and increase speed.
4. Beat in sugar, ¼ cup every 30 seconds.
5. Add vanilla and beat for 2-3 minutes at full speed until very stiff.
6. Remove beaters; fold in additional sugar with spatula - ¼ cup at a time every 30 seconds.
7. Draw 2 - 8" circles on each baking sheet. (You'll have 4 circles altogether).
8. Fill a pastry bag, without a nozzle, with meringue.
9. Pipe the meringue around the four circles making it ½" high and 1" wide. Fill in one circle completely with meringue. This will be the base.
10. Put a star tip on the pastry bag and make 20 flowerettes as decoration. You will have meringue left over. Save it!
11. Put baking sheets in oven and reduce heat to 200°.

— Continued —

12. Bake for 1½ - 2 hours until meringue is completely dry and slides easily off baking sheets.
13. To assemble meringue basket, place baked meringue base on cookie sheet. Pipe additional uncooked meringue on top of outside edge (to act as a glue) and top with one circle of baked meringue. Continue to build basket using all 3 baked circles.
14. Using additional meringue in pastry bag, fill any holes between layers and spread meringue both inside and outside of basket. There must not be any holes. Place 10 flowerettes around edge of basket, using meringue to adhere and 10 flowerettes on sides for decoration. You'll still have meringue left over. Save it.
15. Return assembled basket to 200° oven and bake for another hour or until completely dry.
16. Meanwhile, wash strawberries and set aside 8 for final decoration. Slice the rest.
17. Place sliced berries in a blender with remaining meringue mixture and strawberry liqueur. Puree and refrigerate.
18. Beat cream until it is thick. Refrigerate.
19. When basket is dry and cool, fill with strawberry ice cream; top with cold strawberry meringue mixture. Top again with whipped cream and spread it to edges.
20. Garnish with large whole strawberries.

Serves: 8-10
Preparation: 1 hour
Baking: 2½ hours

This impressive dessert freezes beautifully and is well worth the time and effort. Make it ahead (it will keep for months in a deep freeze) so you can relax and enjoy the "oohs and ahs" of your guests at your next dessert party. (Don't make on a humid day, however, as the meringue won't set.)

VICHYSSOISE (cold)
POTAGE PARMENTIER (hot)
Potato, Leek Soup

A LA - Chez Suzette

3	cups potatoes (peeled and sliced)
3	cups white part of leeks (sliced)
1	qt. water
1	qt. chicken broth
1	T. salt or to taste
⅓	cup whipping cream
1	T. chopped parsley

1. Combine potatoes, leeks, water, broth and salt in four quart saucepan. Cook until potatoes and leeks are tender.
2. Pour small batches into blender or processor and process until smooth.
3. Stir in whipping cream.
4. Refrigerate if serving cold or warm if serving hot.
5. To serve, garnish with parsley.

Serves: 6-8
Preparation: 30 minutes or chill for several hours.

Very good served either way!

Crumpets

Crumpets is the end result of the inspiration and efforts of Anneliese Hutt, a native of Munich, and the current owner, Francois Maeder, a native of Geneva, Switzerland. Crumpets opened in June of 1980.

Unlike many of the other restaurants within these pages, Crumpets' intent is to offer neither haute decor nor haute cuisine. Rather, Francois wishes to provide a very pleasant atmosphere in which to enjoy high quality, fresh foods at a less lofty tariff. Because the cuisine is of such high quality and has elicited so favorable a response, we felt it incumbent upon ourselves to include it in this book.

The atmosphere is a comfortable, at-home variety. Upon entering the brick building, one discovers high ceilings and well-illuminated expanses. Tall plants, modern paintings, and ceiling fans enhance straight-backed blond oak chairs and matching tables.

— Continued —

The cuisine and its preparation evidence Francois's commitment to quality. Everything is fresh, from the popular Pate Maison to the various desserts. A main course of Fresh Green Fettuccine with Scallops, Salad and Bread will exemplify the commitment. Beef Tenderloin, New York Strip Steaks, Baked Red Fish, and several varieties of chicken, including Chicken in Champagne, are all served with the house salad, vegetable of the day, and bread.

Each night a Pot Luck dinner offers the traditional foods of a different country. Live classical music is played nightly.

Crumpets will also provide you with a grand finale of delightful cakes, pies and tarts baked on the premises daily.

Crumpets is located at 5800 Broadway in San Antonio.

STUFFED MUSHROOMS

A LA - Crumpets

12	large mushrooms with stems
1	lemon (juiced)
3	T. butter
⅓	cup shallots (minced)
1	T. lemon juice
1	T. parsley (chopped)
	salt and pepper (to taste)
¼	cup sour cream
3	T. bread crumbs
⅓	cup sausage, salami or hamburger (minced)
⅓	cup fresh grated Parmesan cheese
3	T. scallions (chopped)
6	T. fresh grated cheese (Cheddar, romano, mozzarella or other favorite)

1. Preheat oven to 400°.
2. Remove stems from mushrooms and chop stems. Set aside.
3. Place mushroom caps in bowl, add one cup boiling water and juice from lemon. Let stand one minute. Drain and pat caps dry. Set aside.
4. In a skillet, saute shallots in butter until soft. Add chopped stems, lemon juice and parsley.
5. Remove from heat, add salt and pepper to taste.
6. Stir in sour cream, bread crumbs, minced meat. Let cool.
7. Add Parmesan and scallions.
8. Stuff mushroom caps; garnish with favorite cheese.
9. Bake in greased dish for ten minutes. Serve hot.

Serves: 4 as first course
Preparation: 30 minutes

Delicious! A guaranteed hit for your party.

PATE
(Begin 24 hours in advance)

═══════════════════════════════════

A LA - Crumpets

1	lb. chicken livers
¾	lb. bacon
½	lb. veal or chicken
2	medium onions (peeled)
3	shallots (peeled)
½	t. thyme
1	t. allspice
1	t. coarsely ground pepper
	salt to taste
1	egg
1	T. whipping cream
¼	cup brandy
3	T. parsley
4	bacon slices (Uncooked)
2	bay leaves
1	envelope gelatin

1. Preheat oven to 350°.
2. Grind liver, bacon and veal in food processor until fine.
3. Mince onions and shallots in food processor.
4. Combine onion, shallots and meats. Add spices and seasonings.
5. Beat egg, cream and brandy and add to mixture. Add parsley. Mix well.
6. Line loaf pan or terrine with bacon strips; add 1 bay leaf.
7. Fill with pate mixture and add second bay leaf. Cover.
8. Stand container in pan of hot water. Cook for 1½ - 2 hours in oven at 350°.

— Continued —

52

9.   Remove from oven; cool; cover plate with aluminum foil. Next, weight the pate with a brick or weighted plate.
10.   Refrigerate 24 hours.
11.   Remove weight and carefully unmold onto serving platter.
12.   Prepare gelatin according to package directions and pour over pate. Refrigerate.
13.   Serve when set or refrigerate until ready to use.

Yield: 1 mold 9x4x4". Slice pate about 3/8" thick then slice again in half, to make about 40 slices.

Preparation: 20 minutes
Cooking: 2 hours
Refrigeration: 24 hours

A mild, good tasting pate. Pates are best after refrigerating two days. This is another great party fare you can make ahead. Serve with gourmet cracker rounds.

FLORENTINES
Lace Cookies

A LA - Crumpets

¾	cup heavy cream
2	cups sugar
1	T. honey
3	cups sliced blanched almonds (finely chopped)
3	cups candied fruit (finely diced)
1	T. flour
2	T. egg whites
1	cup whole blanched almonds (garnish)

1. Preheat oven to 425°.
2. Combine cream sugar and honey in saucepan and bring to a boil, stirring constantly.
3. Remove from heat and add remaining ingredients except for **whole** almonds.
4. Spoon onto greased cookie sheet and flatten into round shapes. Press whole almond into center of each cookie as garnish.
5. Bake in oven until light brown, about 10 minutes. Be careful as they burn easily.
6. Remove from cookie sheet and cool.

Yield: 3-4 dozen
Preparation: 30 minutes

A delicious cookie. Chef suggests they can be dipped in chocolate for a wonderful flavor.

BLACK FOREST CAKE

A LA - Crumpets

1	chocolate cake (cut in 3 layers)
½	cup thick chocolate syrup
½	cup kirsch liqueur
2	cups whipping cream
2	T. confectioners sugar
8	oz. frozen sour cherries (thawed) or 1 (16 oz.) can pitted sour cherries (well drained)
¼	cup chocolate chips or other decorettes
¼	cup shaved unsweetened chocolate maraschino cherries for garnish

1. Cut cake into three layers. Separate layers.
2. Lightly soak layers with chocolate syrup and kirsch.
3. Whip cream with confectioners sugar until it holds peaks.
4. Spread first layer with some whipped cream; top with half the cherries.
5. Add second layer and top with some whipped cream and remaining cherries.
6. Top with final layer. Cover sides and top with remaining whipped cream.
7. Use decorettes around sides and shaved chocolate on top.
8. Garnish with cherries if desired. Refrigerate until served.

Serves 6-8
Preparation: 30 minutes

This dessert is wonderful and beautiful to look at.

J. SNITILY 86©

D'Amico

While not having visited every Italian restaurant in Houston, I would be surprised if directed to one with finer cuisine than D'Amico's. Owner Anthony Rao seems possessed with an instinct for providing dining excellence.

D'Amico's interior is very pleasant. A homey, grandmotherly effect is created by lace curtains, brocaded booths, needle-point-backed chairs, tassled hanging table lamps and old family photos.

The service is tailored in black, is professional and consists of three-man teams including captain, sommelier and food waiter.

But the glories of D'Amico's cuisine warrant these few pages. Each course is a thoughtful weave; each meal a tapestry. Chef Tony Rao emphasizes color, texture and composition as well as taste and aroma. Take the cold seafood salad. Dark lettuce leaves buoy the squid's intermittent flashes of pink champagne, the shrimp's subdued orange, the green mussel, the white meat of the crab and the stone-like pigmentation of the clam. The colors seem even richer due to a marinated olive oil and white wine glaze. Called Insalata Fruitti de Mare, it's a mariner's answer to the impressionist's fruit bowl.

The Cappelini Siciliana also deliciously demonstrates Tony's feeling for texture and color. The texture is largely provided by the capellini - or angel hair. Its saffron filaments weave the nest of a fragile bird, coursing through a sauce consisting of fresh tomato, green capers and the burnished surface of eggplant.

— Continued —

A fresh trout was dipped in egg and flour, then sauteed in white wine and lemon. A generous amount of fresh crab crowned the affair, followed by a sprinkling of pine nuts. Delicious, not greasy, it's understandable why Trota al Toto is D'Amico's number one fish entree.

Veal Marsala heads seven selections of veal. Thinly sliced, sauteed in marsala wine and mushrooms, there's a hint of onion and prosciutto. I found this version of a long Classic dish a source of surfeit as well as sublime.

Eighty percent of the meals partaken at D'Amico are accompanied by wine. The selection is reasonably priced and extensive, with half-bottles available.

Like everything else, the pastries are homemade and excellent. The dessert cart bore regal fruit tarts with an almond base, an elegant chocolate cherry cake, cassata, cannoli, poached pears in Chianti and peeled orange in Grand Marnier. Ice cream with Italian macaroons and spumoni sit off stage. I can attest to the glories of Chocolate Cheesecake and Zabaglione with raspberries. The cheesecake was extremely light and creamy with a rich chocolate taste. The Zabaglione was prepared tableside and required no improvement.

D'Amico is frequented by international celebrities, athletes and local loyalists. Its food has been selected to appear before Hollywood cameras, elegant parties and receptions. Centrally located, open for lunch and dinner, D'Amico's cuisine reinforces the notion that the Italians brought cooking from the galley to the gallery, making it the art form that it is today.

D'Amico is located at 2407 Westheimer in Houston.

CAPELLINI SICILIANA
Pasta with Eggplant

A LA - D'Amico

1	medium eggplant (peeled and cubed)
	salt (to taste)
2	T. olive oil
2	cups Italian tomato sauce
3	T. (heaping) fresh Ricotta cheese
2	T. irregularly shaped capers
8	oz. capellini or vermicelli pasta (a very thin spaghetti)

1. Pat dry eggplant cubes with paper towel and salt lightly.
2. Saute until golden brown in olive oil. Set aside.
3. Simmer tomato sauce in a large saute pan for several minutes.
4. Add Ricotta cheese, eggplant and capers. Simmer for 3 or 4 minutes.
5. Cook capellini in 3 quarts salted, boiling water until al dente (tender but firm to the bite). Drain and transfer to a warm serving bowl.
6. Toss pasta with sauce and serve immediately.

Serves: 4-6
Preparation: 20 minutes total

An inexpensive yet tasty accompaniment to any meal.

VITELLA MARSALA
Veal Scallopini Marsala

A LA - D'Amico

8	4 oz. veal scallops * (thinly sliced)
	flour (to dust veal)
2	oz. olive oil
2	T. butter
1	small white onion (finely chopped)
1	oz. prosciutto ham (diced)
¼	lb. mushrooms (thinly sliced) about 1½ cups
2	oz. Marsala wine
	salt and pepper (to taste)
2	T. butter

1. Dredge veal in flour. Shake off excess flour.
2. In a saute pan over medium heat combine olive oil and butter. When hot, saute veal 1 - 2 minutes on each side until all pieces are done. (Add more oil if necessary.) Remove veal to serving platter and keep hot.
3. In same pan, add onion, prosciutto and mushrooms. Saute for 2 minutes. Strain off excess oil (if any).
4. Add Marsala wine, salt and pepper and 2 T. butter.
5. Mix well; pour over veal and serve.

Serves: 4
Preparation: 20 minutes total

* Veal scallops are the long round muscles of the leg of the calf, cut across the grain.

This is so good, one husband ate the entire meal for four! Fast and easy, too!

TROTA AL TOTO

Trout Topped with Crab and Butter Sauce

A LA - D'Amico

1	cup peanut oil
4	4 - 6 oz. filets of trout (it's easiest to have your butcher filet them for you; ask him to remove bones)
1	cup unbleached flour
3	large eggs (beaten)
6	oz. white wine
6	T. butter (or to taste)
12	oz. lump crab meat
	juice of one lemon
¼	cup toasted pine nuts
3	sprigs parsley (stems discarded and leaves finely chopped)
	salt and pepper (to taste - if necessary)
4	lemon wedges in 4 nets tied with bright green ribbon (garnish)

1. Preheat peanut oil in skillet to 250°. (Check oil temperature by sprinkling a few drops of flour into skillet. It will dance on top when oil is hot enough.)
2. Dust fish on all sides with flour. Next dip into beaten egg and then back into flour.
3. Saute fish in oil. After a few seconds turn heat up to medium high. Saute fish 4 minutes on each side or until golden brown.
4. Remove fish to paper towels. Drain peanut oil from pan and return pan to heat; add wine. Turn heat up to reduce the liquid. Lower heat and stir in butter and crab meat. Add remaining ingredients except garnish.
5. Place trout on serving plates; pour sauce over and garnish with lemon wedges.

Serves: 4
Preparation time: 22 minutes total

Lemony-Butter taste for crab and trout.

MASTER CHEESE CAKE
(Best prepared night before for thorough chilling)

A LA - D'Amico

— Crust —

1¼	cups graham cracker crumbs
¼	cup sugar
¼	cup butter (melted)

— Filling Part I —

2	8 oz. pkg. cream cheese (softened)
3	eggs
½	cup sugar
2¼	t. vanilla extract

— Filling Part II —

1	pint carton sour cream
¼	cup sugar
1	T. vanilla (or any flavor you desire or combination of extracts — You can also use less flavoring)

1. Preheat oven to 350°.
2. Mix crust ingredients and line bottom and sides of a 10" greased pie pan or square pan.
3. Beat ingredients for Filling Part I until smooth. Pour into crust and bake at 350° for 30 minutes. Cool for 15 minutes.
4. Turn oven up to 400°.
5. Mix together Filling Part II ingredients and pour evenly and gently onto cake. Bake at 400° for 10 minutes.
6. Cool cake and refrigerate overnight or several hours at least.

— Continued —

Serves: 6 - 8
Preparation: 20 minutes
Baking: 40 minutes
Refrigeration: Preferably overnight

You can be creative with different toppings or extracts, or it's simply wonderful as is!

To make D'Amico's Chocolate Cheesecake simply melt ½ cup semisweet chocolate chips in top of double boiler and pour over filling Part II in step 5 and bake as directed.

J. SNITILY 86 ©

Durham House

Forty-five minutes south of Dallas, in the rich blacklands of Ellis County, sits the town of Waxahachie and The Durham House. Of less than 20,000 inhabitants, Waxahachie is a repository of nineteenth century Victorian homes that reflect the affluence of those who dealt in cotton.

Mr. Durham built his two-story Victorian frame in 1904 and resided there for the next thirty-five years. The home was rescued from decay by its present owners in 1975. Its lead crystal windows obviate caring and its kempt landscape and spotless front porch earn admiring glances from townsfolk and visitors.

Within its doors lurks neither pretension, gimmicks nor themes. Its inhabitants only wish to provide good food, comfort and pleasant surroundings. Bob Welsh runs the dining and reception area while Jerry Weber handles the kitchen. Their only request is for reservations and prompt arrivals.

Any deviation from the above simplicities would be the decor. The entry hall and side parlors provide a composition that encompasses Early American, Flemish, Victorian, Czarist, Edwardian, abstract and contemporary. The chandeliers alone include an antique French bronzedore with baccarat crystal, a Russian Regency and an Olde English gas version. A large, four-paneled Edwardian screen and a rich tapestry embellish one of the parlors. Even the powder room was found deserving of a crystal, brass and pewter aquarium of Victorian vintage.

— Continued —

65

Leaving the entry hall's white pillars and varnished floor, Bob guided me to one of the parlors and a corner table. Upon being seated before an attractive setting of Noritake china in a Ming Garden pattern, Bob's sister, Louise, provided the menu. The entrees favor beef, but also listed seafood, duck and lamb. I selected Pork Chops Veronique. The "Double pork chops, two inches thick, baked in Frangelica Liqueur, honey, sesame seeds and white grapes" were most impressive. Truly a meal worthy of recall, the wonderfully glazed chops arrived in a quantity only Texas would find non-excessive.

Included with the entree was a tangy Peanut Bisque, a vegetable, rolls and a generous spinach salad with tomato and cucumber.

As I began to review the dessert selections, diners at another table were extolling the virtues of Boccone Dolce, "a nest of French meringue and chocolate, strawberries and Grand Marnier, whipped cream and almonds." I weighed the merits of Peaches Melba, "Peaches, French vanilla ice cream, Chambord Raspberry sauce and whipped cream." I said "Yes" and suffered no regrets, only thoughts of encores. If sweets pique your fancy, I'll conclude with Nocello-Parfait, "French walnut spice cake, black walnut ice cream, glaze of Nocello walnut liqueur, whipped cream and walnuts."

I know that some of you must be pulling your ear and saying that a "Bob" and "Jerry" just do not seem capable of much more than eggs and hash browns. I can assure you that all of the above divinities are their creation.

Open Thursday through Sunday, evenings only, the plains south of Dallas can revive one's spirit and The Durham House will amply reward a hunger for more.

Durham House is located at 603 North Rogers in Waxahachie.

PORK CHOPS VERONIQUE

A LA - Durham House

4	center cut pork chops 2" thick
	salt and pepper (to taste)
½	cup sesame seeds
½	cup water
½	cup white wine
½	cup honey
¼	cup Frangelica liqueur (a hazelnut liqueur)
4	small clusters seedless grapes
4	thin lemon slices (twisted)

1. Preheat oven to 350°.
2. Salt and pepper both sides of pork chops. Place in shallow baking pan.
3. Press sesame seeds in tops of chops.
4. Add water and wine to pan.
5. Bake for 1 hour and 30 minutes or longer, until done.
6. Remove from pan and keep warm.
7. Blend honey and Frangelica liqueur together for glaze. Set aside. (If honey has crytallized, heat it first and then add liqueur)
8. Place warm chops on four plates and garnish with grapes and lemon twists.
9. Spread glaze on top and serve.

Serves: 4
Preparation: 15 minutes
Cooking: 1 hour 30 minutes to 1 hour 45 minutes

Super dish. Makes pork chops a festive fare!

PEACHES MELBA
(Begin 4 hours ahead)

═══════════════════════════════════

A LA - Durham House

2	8 oz. cans sliced freestone peaches or 2 cups fresh peaches if available
½	cup peach brandy
1	8 oz. jar raspberry preserves
1	8 oz. can raspberries or 1 cup frozen raspberries (thawed and drained)
½	cup Chambord raspberry liqueur
1 - 2	drops red food coloring (optional)
½	gallon vanilla ice cream
½	pt. whipping cream (whipped)
4	T. toasted almonds

1. Marinate peaches in brandy at least 4 hours or overnight.
2. In food processor blend raspberry jam, raspberries and Chambord liqueur. Add food coloring if desired. Chill.
3. To serve, place 2 scoops vanilla ice cream in champagne glass. Add marinated peaches; drizzle with Chambord sauce.
4. Garnish with whipped cream and almonds. Serve immediately.

Serves: 4
Preparation time: 20 minutes
Marinate: at least 4 hours or overnight

Wonderful dessert to end a special meal! Easy to do!

The Mandalay
Four Seasons Hotel

Enjolie, at the Mandalay Four Seasons Hotel, must certainly rank as one of Dallas' very finest restaurants. While the cuisine is the focus of this restaurant's efforts, the atmosphere is also very soothing. Unobtrusive, classical music wends its way through the soft lights and dignified furnishings. Lightly toned wood complements warm greens and subdued yellows.

Soon after being seated at dinner, assorted puff pastries will appear and provide sustenance while one peruses the menu.

A dozen hot and cold hors d'oeuvres include Pheasant Mousse with Blueberry Sauce; Smoked Scottish Salmon and Stuffed Quail on Candied Endives in a crepe. Luncheon counterparts include Duck Galantine with Goose Liver and Salad.

A variety of dinner salads utilize duck liver pate, apples, roasted goat cheese, endive, mushrooms, avocados, spinach and walnut dressing. Luncheon salads are headed by Fresh Fruit with Honey and Yogurt Dressing.

Soups offer such rare finds as Lobster Consomme with Fine Champagne; Mussel Soup with Saffron; and Avocado Cream with Crabmeat.

— Continued —

The entrees will live up to your expectations. Braised Dover Sole with Chive Sauce is simple sustenance of the highest order. Roasted Filet of Veal with Mustard Seed Sauce and Boneless Rack of Lamb in Pastry with Spinach, Pleurottes and Herbs witness simplicity and creativity.

For dessert, homemade chocolate, strawberry and pistachio ice creams resting atop a pool of raspberry sauce with a kiwi garnish should entice even the wary.

Whether you partake in lunch or dinner, Enjolie's entire staff accomplishes the sometimes difficult task of being both totally attentive and discreet. Along with their crisp attire, Enjolie will leave you with nothing but positive impressions.

The Mandalay Four Seasons is located at 221 S. Las Colinas Blvd. in Irving.

LA SALADE "ENJOLIE"

A LA - Enjolie

1½ T. wine vinegar
1   t. Dijon mustard
     salt and pepper (to taste)
½   cup walnut oil

2   heads Belgium endive or 2 hearts of romaine lettuce
1   head Bibb lettuce
½   lb. green beans (cooked crisp and cut in 1" slices)
2   apples (Julienned) *
1   t. lemon juice
½   lb. duck liver pate or country pate (cut into thin, French fry-like strips)

1. Combine vinegar, mustard, salt and pepper. Mix well. Slowly whip oil into mixture. Set dressing aside.
2. On four large salad plates, arrange endive leaves in a star pattern, allowing five per plate.
3. Place Bibb lettuce leaves between endive.
4. Arrange green beans in middle of plate and put apple slices on top. Sprinkle with lemon juice.
5. Arrange pate, placing one small piece in each endive leaf. Just before serving pour dressing over top of salad.

Serves: 4
Preparation: 10 minutes

* Leave peel on and cut apples into very thin slices.

An unusual combination that is delightful. Makes a great luncheon salad or first course.

CREME DE TOMATE AUX CUISSES DE GRENOUILLE

Cream of Tomato Soup with Frog Legs

A LA - Enjolie

1	medium onion (diced)
½	stalk celery (diced)
1	small carrot (diced)
1½	T. butter
2	lb. very ripe fresh tomatoes (quartered)
1	clove garlic (chopped)
1	branch fresh thyme or ½ t. dried
2	leaves fresh basil or ½ t. dried
	pinch of sugar
2½	cups chicken stock
4	sets frog legs (1 lb. approximately) removed from bone and diced
2	T. butter
¼	cup whipping cream
	salt and pepper (to taste)
1½	T. butter
2	T. chopped chives

1. In a 4 qt. casserole combine onion, celery and carrot with 1½ T. butter and 2 T. water. Cook over medium low heat until water evaporates. Do not brown vegetables.
2. Add tomato quarters, garlic, thyme, basil and sugar. Cook 5 minutes.
3. Add chicken stock and simmer for 10 min.
4. In a separate pan, saute diced frog legs in 2 T. butter and set aside.
5. Remove thyme branch from soup. Puree soup in blender or processor and strain.

— Continued —

6. Boil remaining soup an additional minute. Add cream; season to taste with salt and pepper. Add remaining butter. Stir.
7. To serve, garnish with diced frog legs and chives. Serve immediately.

Serves: 4
Preparation: 35 minutes

An elegant soup!

CARRE D'AGNEAU EN CROUTE AUX PLEUROTTES

Boneless Rack of Lamb in Pastry
with Spinach, Pleurottes and Herbs

A LA - Enjolie

— Sauce —

	lamb rack bones
½	carrot (diced)
½	onion (diced)
2	T. oil
1	t. flour
½	cup white wine
1	beef bouillon cube
1½	cups water

— Rack of Lamb —

2	boneless racks of lamb (have butcher save bones for you; use in sauce)
	salt and pepper (to taste)
	pinch Herbs de Provence *
1	T. oil
½	lb. sliced pleurottes or shitake mushrooms
1	T. shallot onion (chopped)
1	T. parsley (chopped)
1	T. butter
1	cup spinach (chopped)
	salt and papper (to taste)
1	lb. puff pastry (your bakery will have this, or purchase in frozen food section)
¼	lb. goose liver pureed (or use smooth goose liver pate) - purchase in gourmet section
1	egg (beaten)

— Sauce —

1. Cut bones in pieces. Place in saucepan with carrot, onion and oil. Cook until golden brown.

— Continued —

74

2. Add flour; stir until flour is slightly colored.
3. Add wine and stir to loosen any pieces clinging to pan. Cook until reduced by one half.
4. Add bouillon cube and water. Simmer for one hour.
5. Strain through cheesecloth; season with salt and pepper. Keep warm

— Rack of Lamb —

1. Preheat oven to 450°.
2. Season racks with salt and pepper and Herbs de Provence.
3. Heat pan with oil and sear meat three minutes on each side. Keep meat rare. Remove meat and set aside.
4. Saute mushrooms, shallots and parsley in butter. Add spinach and salt and pepper to taste. Set aside.
5. Roll puff pastry to measure 10 inches long, 8 inches wide and ¼ inch thick. **
6. Spread goose liver puree over meat and place side by side in center of pastry. Cover meat with spinach mushroom mixture.
7. Fold pastry around meat like an envelope, sealing all seams with egg. Place seam sides down on cookie sheet. Brush surface with egg wash.
8. Bake in oven until crust is golden brown, about 10 minutes. Slice and serve hot with lamb sauce.

Serves: 4 - 6
Preparation: 1 hour 25 minutes
Bake: 10 minutes or more, depending on oven.

* Purchase in a gourmet or spice store - or substitute thyme.
**You can save a little dough to make decorations on top of pastry - hearts, flowers and leaves, etc.

A delicious combination — a real party fare!

75

DACQUOISE DESSERT
(Begin several hours ahead)

═══════════════════════════════════════

A LA - Enjolie

— Meringues —

6	egg whites
10	T. sugar
1	T. vanilla extract
¾	cup toasted hazelnuts (finely ground)
1	T. cornstarch
2	T. sugar

— Mocha Cream —

¾	cup half and half cream
3	egg yolks
1¼	cup powdered confectioners sugar
¾	lb. butter (softened)
3	T. instant coffee mixed with 1 T. water
	powdered sugar (garnish)

1. Preheat oven to 275°.

— Meringues —

2. Beat egg whites until foamy. Slowly add 10 T. sugar while beating until stiff peaks form. Beat in vanilla.
3. In a separate bowl, combine hazelnuts, cornstarch and 2 T. sugar. Mix thoroughly. Gently fold into meringue.
4. On parchment paper, draw two 10" circles and cut out. Place on cookie sheet.
5. Scoop meringue into pastry bag filled with ⅜" tip. Pipe meringue, filling circles.
6. Bake for 1 hour. Cool to room temperature.

— Continued —

— Mocha Cream —

7. Cook half and half to boiling point.
8. Meanwhile, combine yolks and confectioners sugar in mixing bowl and blend.
9. When cream boils, remove from heat and slowly pour into egg yolk mixture, beating constantly.
10. Pour custard back into pan and return to heat.
11. Stirring constantly, cook until custard thickens.
12. Pour custard into mixing bowl and beat at low speed until cool, approximately 10 minutes.
13. Beat in butter (in small pieces) until it is completely absorbed.
14. Beat at high speed until fluffy. Add instant coffee and water mix to complete the mocha butter cream.
15. On cake plate, place one meringue. Spread ⅔ mocha cream to within ½" of edge.
16. Place remaining mocha cream in pastry bag with star tip and pipe decorative border around edge.
17. Gently place second meringue on top and garnish with powdered sugar.
18. Serve immediately or refrigerate as long as 2 hours. Meringue will soften if refrigerated longer. It can also be frozen, but once again, the meringue will be softened.

Serves: 8 - 10
Preparation: 2 hours

An involved recipe, but the results are beautiful and rich!

J. SNITILY 86©

Giorgio's

Located above Lubbock in the Texas Financial Center is Giorgio's, a repository of exceptional cooking, comfort and a commanding view. This diamond in the Lubbock dining scene is a product of the talents and labors of George and Cindy Mayer. Cindy is native to New Jersey; George's roots are in Germany.

George's family possessed culinary talents, and at fourteen George entered one of Europes famed culinary institutes. He immigrated to this country in 1964, found employment aboard a cruise ship and there met Cindy.

Cindy, prior to meeting George, evidenced culinary inclinations. However, after their marriage, Cindy began studying the art of cooking and now oversees the kitchen in Giorgio's while George is General Manager.

Whatever the delegation of responsibilities, the result is a popular dining location that has received plaudits from the local food critics and citizens of Lubbock.

— Continued —

The cuisine might be described as European, with the necessary accommodations made to Texan traditions. However, whether it be prime rib or Chicken Cordon Bleu, everything is fresh and each order is individually prepared.

The appetizers, soups, salads, entrees and desserts seem possessed of a creativity, color and freshness that proves to be a visual as well as nourishing pick-me-up.

Appetizers include Escargots in Mushroom Caps, Iced Shrimp in a sharp cocktail sauce, Hearts of Palm and Artichoke Hearts and a most inviting Spinach Custard Mold.

Soups include Creamy Clam Chowder, Original French Onion with wine, cognac and melted Gruyere and the Cold Strawberry Soup, ideally suited for hot days and white wicker.

Various salads include the popular Asparagus Salad, Caesar Salad and a Boston Leaf Salad. A Spinach Salad is coronated with a warm bacon and onion dressing and a garnish of bacon bits and grated egg.

A partial listing of superb entrees includes Beef Stroganoff, Veal Marsala, Chicken Oscar and fresh seafood specialties.

Desserts are of particular interest to Cindy Mayer and are thought to be uniformly excellent. Chocolate Mousse and Strawberry Romanoff are two of her favorites.

A nice feature of Giorgio's is that those persons who only have limited time for lunch can still partake. During the week, a quick-in-and-out buffet of soup, sandwiches and salads is offered in the lounge area only. The Mayer's attempt to steer clear of dull fare is exemplified in the sandwich selection, fettuccine dishes and low calorie, low sodium items. Particularly popular is the fancy pepper burger with cognac sauce.

George and Cindy Mayer have created a cuisine whose quality and presentation are head and shoulders above that of standard fare. It is only proper their efforts be made in such a lofty locale.

Giorgio's is located at the corner of 19th & University in the Texas Financial Center Bldg. on the 6th floor in Lubbock.

COLD STRAWBERRY SOUP

(Begin at least 3 hours ahead - can be started before)

A LA - Giorgio's

1	**dry qt. fresh strawberries (washed and hulled)**
2	**T. sugar**
3	**T. sugar**
3	**cups plain yogurt**
½	**cup milk**
½	**cup whipping cream**
	fresh mint leaves for garnish

1. Thinly slice strawberries into large bowl and sprinkle with 2 T. of sugar. Mix well and refrigerate for at least 1 hour or as long as overnight.
2. Remove from refrigerator. Place only ¼ cup of berries and remaining 3 T. sugar in blender or processor. Blend until smooth and pour into serving bowl.
3. Blend, in small batches, the remaining berries, yogurt, milk and cream and add to bowl. Stir to mix.
4. Chill at least one hour. Thirty minutes before serving time, remove from refrigerator and garnish.

Serves: 4 as first course
       8 as a light dessert
Preparation: 20 minutes
Refrigeration: at least 2 hours or overnight.

Delicious as either first or last course! Easy!

ASPARAGUS SALAD

A LA -Giorgio's

24   medium thick asparagus

— French Mustard Dressing —

2   T. Dijon mustard
¼   t. salt (or to taste)
¼   t. pepper (or to taste)
3   T. red wine vinegar
½   cup olive oil

2   heads Bibb lettuce
2   T. fresh parsley (chopped)
1   T. green onion, white part only (chopped)
1   hard boiled egg yolk, sieved (garnish)
**   chopped parsley (garnish)**

1.   Peel and trim asparagus. Cut off tips at three inches; cut remaining stalks into ¾" pieces. Tie the tips into two bundles with kitchen string.
2.   Cook all asparagus in large saucepan in salted boiling water, covered, for 5 - 7 minutes or until just tender. Do not overcook.
3.   Carefully lift out tips and drain. Drain remaining asparagus in colander. Remove strings and pat dry.

— French Mustard Dressing —

4.   In a blender combine mustard, salt and pepper to taste and add vinegar.
5.   Slowly add olive oil in a steady stream while blender is on until well combined.

— Continued —

6.   Transfer ½ cup dressing to large bowl and add leaves from Bibb lettuce; add chopped parsley and onion. Toss.
7.   In another bowl, carefully coat asparagus with remaining dressing.
8.   On individual salad plates, arrange leaves hollow side up; add asparagus pieces and top the salad with tips. Garnish with yolk and parsley.

Serves: 4 - 6
Preparation: 15 minutes

So easy and elegant! A delicious alternative for salad when guests are coming!

CHICKEN SUPREME WESSEX

A LA - Giorgio's

4 - 6   chicken breasts*

— Sauce —

1	**large bell pepper (Julienne cut)****
2	**T. onion (chopped)**
1	**T. butter or margarine**
2	**T. brandy**
2	**artichoke bottoms - canned or fresh cooked (Julienne cut)****
2	**cups heavy cream**
½	**t. salt**
¼	**t. white pepper**
4	**tomatoes (chopped)**
20 -	**24 frozen shrimp (thaw and pat dry)**
1	**T. cornstarch mixed with 1 T. cold water**

1. Poach chicken breasts in water for eight minutes or until done. Set aside and keep hot.

— Sauce —

2. Saute pepper and onion in butter until soft. Do not brown.
3. Add brandy. Tilt pan. Ignite with match and flambe.
4. After flame dies, add artichokes and cook 1 minute.
5. Stir in cream, salt and pepper and cook 5 more minutes.
6. Add tomatoes and shrimp and heat thoroughly.
7. Add cornstarch and water. Cook until thickened. If it becomes too thick, add a little more water (1 - 3 teaspoons).

— Continued —

84

8.   Place cooked chicken breasts in individual casserole dishes which have been heated. Pour sauce over breasts and serve.

Serves: 4 - 6
Preparation: 25 minutes

* Also excellent sauce for fish fillets!
** Very thin French fry-like strips

Pretty, delicious and easy for your next dinner party!

VEAL MEDALLION A LA CREME

A LA - Giorgio's

— Sauce —

¼	cup butter or margarine
2	cups mushrooms (thinly sliced)
¼	cup green onions (chopped)
½	cup Tawny Port wine
2	t. cornstarch mixed with 4 t. water
2	cups heavy cream
½	t. salt
¼	t. white pepper
8	veal medallions (¼" thick)
	flour (to dust)
	butter and corn oil (to saute)
	parsley (fresh chopped - for garnish)

— Sauce —

1. Melt butter in skillet and saute mushrooms. Remove mushrooms and set aside until later. Saute onions several minutes until limp in same pan.
2. Add Tawny Port. Cook until liquid is reduced to ¼ cup.
3. Next, add cornstarch-water mixture. Stir in cream and cook until thick and smooth.
4. Add salt and pepper and adjust to taste.
5. Add mushrooms. Cover pan and set aside. Keep warm.
6. Pound veal to ¼" thickness. Dust with flour.
7. Saute in equal parts butter and corn oil for 3 minutes on each side or until done.
8. Top with sauce and garnish with parsley.

Serves: 4 - 6
Preparation: 25 minutes

The Tawny Port gives this dish a most wonderful flavor!

MOUSSE AU CHOCOLATE

A LA - Giorgio's

5	oz. semi-sweet chocolate
2	cups boiling water
7	medium eggs
3	T. Grand Marnier liqueur
1	cup whipping cream (whipped)
	grated chocolate (garnish)

1. Break up chocolate and place in large bowl. Pour two cups of boiling water over chocolate and allow to melt. Do not mix.
2. Separate eggs. Beat whites until stiff.
3. Put yolks in a medium bowl with liqueur.
4. Drain water off and add melted chocolate to yolks. Mix thoroughly.
5. Gently fold beaten whites into chocolate mixture, one third at a time, until just blended.
6. Immediately scoop into 6 dessert glasses. Cover and refrigerate several hours.
7. Garnish with whipped cream and grated chocolate.

Serves: 6
Preparation: 20 minutes
Refrigeration: 3 or more hours

Very easy, and no added sugar!

J. SNITILY 86 ©

Green Pastures

Though within Austin's city limits, Green Pastures appears but a step from the country. Its neighborhood of nicely spaced modest homes, trees, grass and narrow, winding road instill a feeling somewhere outside an urban spectre.

Built in 1894, the two-story, white Victorian residence sits on five-plus acres that nurture over 130 live oak, bamboo, magnolia, cedar, pomegranate and support trellis work upon which climb the yellow flower of the Carolina Jasmine. Several out-structures include the gazebo which has witnessed many a wedding, the Old Well House which now stores wine and the White House which handles the catering service. A dozen peacodks provide additional color, while a rooster, bluejays and various song birds note their enthusiasm.

Crossing a veranda of gray wood decking and ceiling of shoe-fly blue, I entered the front door on a Sunday at noon. There was quite a gathering for the Sunday Buffet. Voices of all ages engaged in conversation and melded into uniform enthusiasm and levity.

The interior's detail, workmanship and materials won my attention. Louisiana pine and cypress showcased the reception area and private dining rooms. Chimney mantles of birds-eye maple and oak, Oriental rugs, various antiques and stained glass windows were all within view under the twelve foot ceilings.

The Cotillion Room is the focal point for the Sunday Buffet. Spacious, light, white and airy, it seemed swathed in a saffron hue. French doors along two walls lead to the popular Sunporch and Gallery. Blue fabriced chairs set off rose-colored tablecloths, fanned napkins, petite flower arrangements and

— Continued —

sparkling services. The buffet table ran the middle of the floor, and perpendicular to it, along one wall, the dessert table.

My trip along the buffet table taxed the limits of my plate. Entrees of Prime Rib and Swordfish with Garlic Butter were preceded by the delicious Asparagus Mold, sliced fresh fruit in their natural juices, Ricotta Filled Mushroom Caps, Chantilly Potatoes and Apple Filled Yellow Squash to name only some of the offerings.

The in-house bakery made a variety of breads and rolls including both herb and tomato and pumpkin and apricot muffins.

The dessert table offered an imposing Lemon Roll, Chocolate Mousse, Strawberry Parfait, Brownies and Texas Ranger Cookies that contained ample amounts of walnuts and coconut. One is also likely to encounter Green Pastures Cheesecake, Coconut Buttermilk Pie, Peach Cobbler and Apple-Walnut Pie.

The full service bar area, besides creating the delicious Milk Punch, makes available a wide variety of wines, including the increasingly popular Texas wines. The Texas Wine Room, located on the second floor of Green Pastures, provides further insight into this relatively new and very interesting Texan enterprise.

An extremely adept and crisply attired staff brings the above mentioned delights to your table. Always within view, yet never obtrusive, the diner's needs seem the sole focus of their attentions.

An institution since 1945, Green Pastures is intent on maintaining a tradition for excellent food, a most pleasant atmosphere and genuine hospitality. Open seven days a week for lunch, dinner and the Sunday Buffet, I would encourage everyone within the Hill Country to consider Green Pastures' substantial offerings.

Green Pastures is located at 811 West Live Oak St. in Austin.

MOLDED GAZPACHO SALAD

A LA - Green Pastures

1	envelope unflavored gelatin dissolved in ¼ cup water
1½	cups hot tomato juice
6	large ripe tomatoes (peeled, seeded and finely chopped)
1	cucumber (peeled and finely chopped)
⅓	cup green pepper (chopped and blanched)*
⅛	t. tabasco sauce
4	T. olive oil
1½	T. red wine vinegar
1	t. salt
¼	t. white pepper
1	T. green onion (chopped)
1	clove garlic (minced)
½	cup mayonnaise
½	cup celery (diced)

1. Combine dissolved gelatin and hot tomato juice. Refrigerate to partially gel.
2. Combine remaining ingredients except mayonnaise and celery. Add to partially gelled juice.
3. Pour into individual molds that have been greased with mayonnaise or Pam.
4. Refrigerate until set. Unmold and garnish with mayonnaise mixed with diced celery.

Serves: 6 - 8
Preparation: 30 minutes

*To blanch the peppers, put them in boiling water for two minutes, then quickly submerge in an ice bath.

A refreshing warm weather salad. Perfect with seafood or cold cuts.

ASPARAGUS MOLD
(Begin several hours ahead)

A LA - Green Pastures

1   can (15 ½ ozs.) green asparagus pieces
1   cup hot liquid (juice from asparagus)
1   envelope gelatin, dissolved in ¼ cup cold water
½   cup mayonnaise
½   cup sour cream
1   t. salt
2   T. lemon juice
1   cup blanched almonds (chopped)
1   head Bibb lettuce or leaf lettuce

1.   Heat liquid from asparagus and pour over dissolved gelatin (add water if necessary to equal 1 cup liquid).
2.   Cool in refrigerator until partially set.
3.   Fold in mayonnaise, sour cream, salt and lemon juice.
4.   Add asparagus and almonds.
5.   Pour into individual molds and chill until well set.
6.   Serve on lettuce leaves.

Serves: 6 - 8
Preparation: 15 minutes
Refrigeration: at least one hour

This is a wonderfully delicious salad! Perfect for luncheons!

SAUCE ANNA MARIA
For Veal or Chicken

A LA - Green Pastures

2   t. butter
1   shallot (finely chopped)
2   T. crushed green peppercorns (find in relish or gourmet
       section of grocery)
5   medium mushrooms (sliced thinly)
1½   cups dry white wine
1½   cups whipping cream

1.   Melt butter in skillet. Briefly saute: shallot, peppercorns
       and mushrooms.
2.   Add wine and cook until reduced by half.
3.   Add cream and reduce by half again.
4.   Serve over veal or chicken.

Serves: 6 - 8
Preparation: 45 minutes

Yield: 1¼ cups sauce.
Serves: 4 (allow approximately ¼ cup per serving)

**This sauce makes any cut of chicken special and veal
outstanding!**

CHICKEN PICATTA

A LA - Green Pastures

6   chicken breasts (boned)
      butter (to saute)

— Picatta Sauce —

¾   cup dry white wine
¼   cup white wine vinegar
1½   t. garlic (finely minced)
¼   cup shallots (finely minced)
¾   t. white pepper
1½   cups butter (cut into small chunks)
⅛   cup crushed drained capers

1.   Saute chicken breasts in butter until done, about 5-10
      minutes. Keep hot.

— Picatta Sauce —

2.   In a small saucepan, combine wine, wine vinegar, garlic
      and shallots. Cook until reduced * by slightly more than
      one half.
3.   Remove from heat. Add pepper and allow to cool
      slightly.
4.   Gradually incorporate butter by adding it in small
      chunks, one at a time, using a whisk to beat it. As one
      chunk begins to dissolve, add another, whisking con-
      stantly. Do not allow butter to melt and separate.
5.   Strain out garlic and shallots and add capers.
6.   Serve Picatta Sauce over chicken breasts.

Serves: 6
Preparation: 45 minutes

* See Glossary under Reduce for additional information
if necessary.
A delicious sauce for chicken!

94

COCONUT BUTTERMILK PIE

A LA - Green Pastures

6	**eggs**
1¾	**cups sugar**
3	**T. flour**
3	**T. vanilla**
½	**cup buttermilk**
	pinch of salt
1	**9" unbaked pastry shell**
1	**cup coconut**

1. Preheat oven to 325°.
2. Beat the eggs well.
3. Add sugar and flour and mix well, making sure there are no lumps.
4. Add vanilla, buttermilk and salt; mix well.
5. Pour mixture into pie shell.
6. Top with coconut.
7. Bake until pie is brown, puffed up and firm, about 45 - 60 minutes.

Serves: 6 - 8
Preparation: 15 minutes
Baking time: 45 - 60 minutes

This is a marvelous pie! Light and very tasty! Very easy, too!

GREEN PASTURES CHEESECAKE

A LA - Green Pastures

— Crust —

¾	cup graham cracker crumbs
3	T. sugar
¼	cup butter (melted)

— Cake —

3	lbs. cream cheese
2	t. vanilla
1½	cups sugar
4	eggs

— Topping —

1	lb. sour cream
¼	cup sugar
	juice from ½ lemon
	juice from ½ lime

1. Preheat oven to 350°.
2. Combine crust ingredients and pat into bottom of 10 inch springform pan.
3. Combine cream cheese and vanilla and beat until smooth, scraping bowl three times.
4. Add sugar and continue to beat and scrape bowl.
5. Add eggs one at a time while beating mixture.
6. Scrape bowl and beat again until there are no lumps.
7. Pour mixture over crust mixture.
8. Bake in oven for one hour and 15 minutes.
9. Remove from oven and let cool.
10. Combine topping ingredients. Mix well.

— Continued —

11. Pour on top of baked, cooled cheesecake.
12. Bake in 350° oven for twenty additional minutes.
13. Remove and cool.

Serves: 10 - 12
Preparation: 30 minutes
Baking: 1 hour 35 minutes
Cooling: Several hours in refrigerator is best.

This is a delicious creamy rich cake. Makes any occasion special.

MILK PUNCH

A LA - Green Pastures

3	ozs. bourbon
1½	ozs. rum
1	oz. brandy
1	cup vanilla ice cream
2	ozs. half and half
2	dashes of nutmeg

1. Into blender pour bourbon, rum and brandy. Add ice cream and half and half.
2. Blend.
3. Pour into glasses and sprinkle with nutmeg.

Serves: 2
Preparation: 5 minutes

Enjoy!

Hunan 湖南樓

a James Huang Restaurant

It has been said that the Chinese have historically treated their cuisine with an uncommon respect. In traditional Chinese kitchens, foods were cut, shredded and diced rather than hacked and torn. Uniform serving bowls accorded each foodstuff its own identity.

James Huang, owner of Hunan, went into none of the above as he discussed the keen competition among Houston's restaurateurs. But as the various selections were brought to our table, my thoughts turned to China, its cultures and the apparent respect these cultures developed for that primary and, too often, scarce necessity.

For the moment let us leave the table and pinpoint our location. Hunan is located on Houston's fashionable Post Oak Boulevard, between San Felipe and Westheimer. Parking is usually available in the large shaded lot located within an egg roll of the glass doors. Both exterior and interior are done in a style that more than meets the requirements of this high rent district. Very attractive jade-like marble walls accent an expansive white soffit and modest, but well kept, hedge.

Upon entering, the staff's competence, equanimity and precision will momentarily rival decor for your attention. It's difficult, however, to ignore the red upholstered walls which support grandiose and more modest bronze murals, an exquisite needlepoint tapestry and paintings. Interior window boxes contain healthy plants and rich red drapes are gathered at window ends. Upholstered armchairs and red leather-like banquettes flank tables attired in white linen and very beautiful chinaware that displays a bright floral pattern over ebony.

— Continued —

The province of Hunan is in South Central China and the word Hunan means "South of the Lake", the lake being Tung Ting Lake. Hunan has a temperate climate, an abundance of mineral resources and varied crops including rice and tea. Although regional cooking is increasingly difficult to classify, Hunan and Szechwan cooking are more inclined to use spices such as red and green peppers, wild peppercorns and cinnamon.

Mr. Huang offers a fare that is hotter and spicier than either Mandarin or Cantonese due to the use of a special red pepper. An extremely diverse menu clearly identifies those items that are hot and spicy. It might be pointed out that Mr. Huang uses that red pepper in moderation and those diners who enjoy their food truly hot and spicy should so stipulate.

Over seventy-five menu items provide ample opportunity to mix hot and spicy with the mild. A mild Velvet Corn Soup with crabmeat began my trek and was followed by an entree of Hunan Prawns that were sauteed in fresh garlic, ginger and the Hunan hot sauce. A more conservative tact might begin with hot and sour Hunan soup and then move on to Empress Tsu-Shi's Shrimp — a mingling of shrimp, broccoli, ham, bamboo shoots and mushrooms in a white sauce. Although Tsu-Shi was the most powerful empress in Chinese history, her namesake possesses a mild disposition. "Happy Family" brought before me sliced prawns, breast of chicken and pork sauteed with crisp vegetables in the Hunan sauce.

Hot and cold appetizers are more than twelve in number and include Diced Boneless Squab, Shrimp Toast and Honey Crisp Walnuts.

The dessert menu offers Chilled Lichees, the Honey Crisp Banana and ice cream.

Whether it be the guiding hand of one's cultural heritage or the more immediate demands of competition, James Hunan is genteel and obviously accords his food a respect that has translated into a large following and very few leftovers.

Hunan is located at 1800 Post Oak Boulevard in Houston.

CREAMED CORN SOUP

A LA - Hunan

3	cups chicken stock or chicken broth
4	oz. creamed style canned corn
3	egg whites (beaten until just frothy)
1	t. salt (optional)
1	t. cornstarch
1	t. water
5	oz. fresh crabmeat

1. Heat chicken stock and corn together in saucepan.
2. When hot, pour in egg whites and salt and stir.
3. Combine cornstarch and water to add to soup. Cook and stir until soup thickens.
4. Divide crabmeat among four soup bowls.
5. Pour hot soup over crab and serve immediately.

Serves: 4
Preparation: 20 minutes

A good first course to an Oriental meal!

TSU SHI SHRIMP

A LA - Hunan

½	lb. jumbo shrimp (peeled, deveined and sliced in two, lengthwise)
2	egg whites
1	t. cornstarch
½	t. salt
1	cup oil
¼	cup snow peas
¼	cup bamboo shoots (sliced)
¼	cup broccoli (chopped)
¼	cup watercress
¼	cup mushrooms (sliced)
1	clove garlic (finely chopped)
1	small piece fresh ginger (finely chopped)
½	cup chicken stock
2	t. white wine
½	t. cornstarch
1	t. sesame oil

1. Beat egg whites and cornstarch with salt until stiff. Set aside.
2. In a wok or deep pan, heat oil until very hot, almost to smoking (about 5 minutes).
3. Combine shrimp and egg white and coat well.
4. To wok add shrimp, peas, bamboo shoots, broccoli, watercress and mushrooms. Cook, stirring constantly, until shrimp is barely pink, approximately 1 - 2 minutes.

— Continued —

5. Remove shrimp and vegetables from oil with slotted spoon and keep warm.
6. In separate pan saute garlic and ginger in very little oil. Add chicken stock and wine mixed with cornstarch, and cook until thickened.
7. Add sesame oil and pour sauce over shrimp and vegetables.

Serves: 2
Preparation: 25 minutes

A delicate combination of shrimp and vegetables!

HUNAN PRAWNS

A LA - Hunan

¼	cup ketchup
1	T. soy sauce
2	t. sugar
1	t. vinegar
2	T. salad oil
½	lb. jumbo shrimp (peeled and deveined)
4	t. onion (finely chopped)
1	t. ginger root (finely chopped)
1	t. garlic (finely chopped)

1. Combine ketchup, soy sauce, sugar and vinegar in small bowl.
2. Mix well and set aside.
3. Heat oil in saute pan over medium high heat.
4. Add shrimp and saute for 2 - 3 minutes until almost done.
5. Add onion, ginger and garlic. Saute one minute longer.
6. Pour sauce ingredients over shrimp and cook for one minute.
7. Serve immediately!

Serves: 2
Preparation: 10 minutes

A quick entree that's very good!

CRISPY BANANAS

A LA - Hunan

4	small bananas, firm and still slightly green
1	cup cornstarch
2	egg whites
1	T. sugar
½	cup water
1	cup vegetable oil
1	cup sugar
½	cup honey
	oil to coat serving dishes
	small bowl with 1 cup water and 1 cup ice cubes

1. Cut bananas in quarters or eighths.
2. Combine cornstarch, egg whites, sugar and water to make a thick batter.
3. Heat oil in wok or deep pan over high heat.
4. While oil is heating, combine sugar and honey in a separate saucepan and cook until very hot.
5. Coat 4 dessert plates with a little oil. Set aside.
6. Dip bananas in cornstarch batter until well coated.
7. Fry several pieces at a time for approximately 30 seconds or until just golden brown. Remove and drain. Fry again for 30 seconds and drain.
8. Dip fried pieces in hot sugar/honey mixture.
9. Next plunge in ice cube water. Coating will harden.
10. Arrange on dessert plates and serve immediately. Don't burn your tongue!

Serves: 4
Preparation: 20 minutes

A little tricky. Helps to have extra set of hands. Unusual ending to dinner.

J. SNITILY 86 ©

The INN at Brushy Creek

The Inn at Brushy Creek is located seventeen miles north of Austin in Round Rock. A large round rock still sits quite conspicuously in the shallow waters of Brushy Creek from where it guided wayfarers during the nineteenth century and probably much earlier. Flanking the town on its east and west sides are the Old Shawnee Trail and the Chisholm Trail respectively.

The Inn resides in what was formerly the Cole residence, a one story structure built within several hundred yards of Brushy Creek in 1842.

The Inn's co-owners and founders, Fred Tinin and Buzz Kelly, decided early on that their restaurant would feature neither traditional Texas fare nor decor, but would reflect the combined tastes of sensitive, knowledgeable, traveled men. A casual air would be maintained by a relaxed dress code and informal service.

In August of 1969, the home's original cypress doors swung open to the public and despite recessions and increased competition, the idea spawned on Cape Cod still sustains itself admirably in South Central Texas.

Shortly after crossing the front porch and entering the reception area, I felt I would enjoy my stay. It was cool and tranquil and the recorded notes of a classical guitar seemed apropos. The furnishings were substantial and of fine aged woods. The many accessory items deserved closer inspection.

— Continued —

I was led to a corner table in one of the three moderately-sized dining rooms. While familiarizing myself with the chair's contours, my eyes turned to the table setting which included a storm lamp, pistol-handled stainless and very attractive Villeroy and Boch china in a basket design. This room's accessories included primitive pieces, still lifes, chalk ware, Early American pottery, willow ware, fireplace equipment and vintage clocks.

The menu listed twelve reasonably priced entrees including sentimental favorites, Tournedos of Beef Henry IV and Trout Dr. Livingston. The former tops two mignons with bearnaise and sauteed mushrooms. The latter incorporates baked, boned trout with bananas and lime hollandaise. I chose Goulibiac of Salmon, a fresh Columbia River salmon, baked with shallots, eggs and hollandaise in a dark brown pastry shell. All entrees included homemade bread, soup, fruit and vegetables. Thickly sliced bread came in a basket, and with whipped butter was truly delicious. The Portuguese soup, a Buzz Kelly creation, was composed of tomato broth, red beans, cabbage and a delicious local sausage. An extremely large salad was served, accompanied by three outstanding dressings. Soon, a large serving bowl of peach halves and sweet gherkins in natural juices arrived; later, side dishes of green beans, cauliflower and carrots.

Fred Tinin is not only the chef and saucier, he is a patissier of consequence. Chocolate Decadence was a fudge cake stuffed with chocolate almond mousse. The Black Russian Pie included kahlua, vodka, whipped cream and a chocolate cookie crust. Ms. Scarlet's Weakness - French vanilla ice cream covered with milk chocolate, Rhett's bourbon, whipped cream and pecans - would prove the undoing of men as well as women. Fresh strawberries in an English custard sauce and Praline Macaroon Cheesecake rounded out the offerings.

Although American wines are stocked, patrons may bring their own wine or alcohol. A per person corkage fee provides an opener, ice-bucket and glasses.

Because the Inn accommodates less than forty-five patrons and is open only Thursday, Friday and Saturday evenings, reservations are essential. The Inn at Brushy Creek is located on IH 35 at the Taylor Exit, Westside Old Town in Round Rock.

PORTUGUESE SOUP

A LA - The Inn at Brushy Creek

3	T. oil
3	cloves garlic (chopped)
1	cup onions (chopped)
½	lb. garlic flavored smoked pork sausage, Elgin type or Linguica. (Cut into bite size pieces)
5	cups beef stock (add more if more broth is desired)
1	15 oz. can kidney beans with liquid
1	small head green cabbage (cored and chopped)
6	small new potatoes (scrubbed and quartered)
3	T. vinegar (more or less to taste)
1	cup catsup
	salt and pepper (to taste)

1. Saute garlic and onions in oil. When the vegetables are just transparent, add sausage slices and brown lightly.
2. Add beef stock and all other ingredients.
3. Bring soup to a boil, stirring to keep the bottom of the pot from burning. Reduce heat.
4. Allow to simmer for 35 to 45 minutes or longer if you like, stirring occasionally. Correct seasonings to taste with salt and pepper.

Yield: 2 quarts
Preparation: 23 minutes
Cooking time: 35 - 45 minutes

This hearty soup freezes well EXCEPT for the potatoes which will disintegrate when the soup is thawed and heated. Flavor of soup is best when it is kept refrigerated for a few days and reheated. Will keep for up to a week in the refrigerator.

TROUT DR. LIVINGSTON

(Trout baked with Banana and topped with Lime Hollandaise Sauce)

A LA - The Inn at Brushy Creek

6	trout fillets (6 - 7 oz. each) (Have butcher fillet them for you if you'd like. It's easier)
¼	cup bread crumbs
6	medium sized ripe bananas

— Lime Hollandaise —

½	lb. (2 sticks) butter (melted)
4	egg yolks
½	t. salt
½	t. dry mustard
	dash of Tabasco
1	T. fresh lemon juice
2	t. fresh lime juice
	Lime slices (garnish)

1. Preheat oven to 450°.
2. Place trout fillets, skin-side down, on ungreased baking sheet. Sprinkle lightly with bread crumbs.
3. Peel bananas; cut each in half; slice each half into 4 lengthwise slices. Overlap slices to cover each fillet completely.
4. Bake for 20 minutes or until fish flakes easily. Meanwhile, prepare Lime Hollandaise Sauce.

— Lime Hollandaise Sauce —

5. Melt butter in small sauce pan. Take care not to burn.
6. Place egg yolks in blender jar with remaining ingredients, except garnish. Blend to mix.

- Continued -

110

7. **Slowly** dribble boiling butter into the yolk mixture on medium-high speed. Use a spatula to keep mixture turning until all butter is incorporated into the Hollandaise sauce.

8. When fish is done, insert spatula between fillet and skin; fillet will separate from tough skin. Place skinned fillet on serving dish.
9. Top with Lime Hollandaise; garnish with lime slices, and serve immediately. *

Serves: 6
Preparation: 20 minutes
Baking time: 20 minutes

* Hollandaise can be kept warm over hot (NOT BOILING) water or in a wide-mouth Thermos bottle.

You would never think to combine trout with bananas, and yet this is the most delicious trout dish we've tasted! Try it for sure!!

CHOCOLATE TRUFFLE TORTE

A LA - The Inn at Brushy Creek

— Torte —

1	12 oz. pkg. semi-sweet chocolate chips
6	T. unsalted butter
2	T. vanilla (do not use vanilla flavored substitute)
3	extra large egg yolks (room temperature)
2	t. flour
2	T. sugar
3	extra large egg whites (room temperature)
	pinch of salt

— Topping —

1	3 oz. pkg. cream cheese (room temperature)
½	cup sugar
1	T. pure vanilla
¼	t. almond extract
1	cup heavy whipping cream
	toasted sliced almonds or chopped pecans (optional - garnish)

1.   Preheat oven to 425°.

— Torte —

2.   Melt chocolate with butter and vanilla in double boiler.
3.   Gradually beat egg yolks into the semi-cooled chocolate mixture until well mixed.
4.   Add flour and sugar and beat until well mixed.
5.   In separate bowl, beat egg whites with salt until stiff. Do not overbeat.

— Continued —

6. Gently fold beaten egg whites into chocolate mixture. Do not overfold mixture. Slight traces of egg whites in the batter will not affect the final texture of the torte.
7. Gently pour mixture into an 8-inch buttered springform pan. Place in the center of the preheated oven.
8. Bake 15 minutes. Remove from oven to cool. When properly cooled, the center will be soft to touch.

— Topping —

9. Beat the cream cheese until fluffy.
10. Add sugar, vanilla, and almond extract. Beat until smooth, using a spatula to scrape down the sides of the bowl. Shut off mixer, scrape down sides of bowl.
11. Restart mixer on lowest speed. **Slowly** add the whipping cream. Beat for one minute on low speed, continuing scraping down the sides of the bowl. Increase speed to medium high until mixture is expanded and stiff.
12. Gently spread mixture on top of torte, smoothing the topping out to the edges.
13. Option: If desired, top with toasted sliced almonds or finely chopped pecans.
14. Chill a couple of hours and serve.* Will keep in refrigerator for three to four days if covered.

Serves: 6 - 8 (very rich - use small portions)
Preparation: 35 minutes
Baking time: 15 minutes
Refrigeration: 2 hours or more.*

* This also tastes wonderful cooled to room temperature, if you can't wait for the refrigeration process.

Absolutely delicious and easy! Your guests will rave! Make it!

J. SNIHLY 86©

La Louisiane

San Antonio's La Louisiane ranks as one of the Southwest's most enduring and consistently acclaimed dining establishments. It was opened in 1935 by Max Manus, an immigrant to America by way of Turkey, Greece and France. Since 1958, Max's son-in-law, George Dareos, has continued "La Lou's" reputation for haute cuisine and unexcelled service.

Besides wearing four stars in the Mobil Travel Guide, La Louisiane is one of only six restaurants in the country to win the Holiday Magazine Award for distinctive dining for over thirty-five consecutive years.

Within the elegant interior, Mr. Dareos presides over his staff of forty-seven, including fifteen full-time waiters. In true haute cuisine style, each table is serviced by three members of the staff: the front waiter, the kitchen waiter and the busboy. Such specialization offers many benefits. One needs never ask for water, coffee or butter refills; and the ashtrays and linen never seem to accumulate debris.

Mr. Dareos and Chef Joaquin Gonzales oversee a kitchen that focuses on classic French, Creole and Cajun cooking. The latter two seem best represented among the wide range of appetizers, including Shrimp Remoulade, Creole Gumbo and Crayfish Bisque.

— Continued —

Approximately two dozen entrees represent fish, meat and fowl. The Red Snapper Louisiane and the Chicken Saute will prove worthy choices. The Chicken Marengo is served alongside asparagus, grilled tomato, wild rice, whole mushrooms and artichoke hearts hollandaise. The Steak Diane includes mushrooms and wild rice, prepared tableside.

La Lou's second floor provides live music, dance facilities and an exceptional way to round out a memorable evening.

La Louisiane is located at 2632 Broadway in San Antonio.

TARMOSALATA
Carp Roe Spread (Caviar)

A LA - La Louisiane

6	slices coarse white bread (crust removed)
1	cup cold water
½	cup Tarama (salted carp roe) - these delicious fish eggs are available in delicatessen or gourmet food shops
¼	cup fresh lemon juice
¼	cup onion (finely chopped)
¾ -	1 cup olive oil

1. Soak bread in water for five minutes. Vigorously squeeze bread dry.
2. Combine bread and roe in blender or processor and blend until mixture is smooth.
3. Leave blender running; add lemon juice and onion.
4. Still blending, pour in olive oil in a thin steady stream. Add as much as needed to make a spread thick enough to hold its shape on a spoon.
5. Refrigerate until ready to use. Taramosalata will thicken more as it chills.

Makes: 2 cups
Preparation: 10 minutes

Serve as part of an appetizer platter accompanied by crackers, black bread or light toast and lemon wedges for garnish. Of course, the ideal beverage accompaniment is champagne.

CRESSON DRESSING
(For Salads and Seafoods)

A LA - La Louisiane

½   bunch watercress (stems removed)
5   cloves garlic (chopped)
2   cups mayonnaise
3   lemons (juiced)
     salt and pepper (to taste)

1.   Finely grind watercress and garlic cloves in a blender or processor.
2.   Stir in mayonnaise and lemon juice and season to taste with salt and pepper.
3.   Refrigerate until serving.

Serves: 6
Preparation: 10 minutes

A subtle blend of flavors. Used on salads or served with cold seafood.

OYSTERS KILPATRICK

A LA - La Louisiane

— **Kilpatrick Sauce** —

1½	**cups chili sauce**
1½	**cups catsup**
1	**stalk celery (finely chopped)**
3	**t. Worcestershire sauce**
3 -	**6 drops Tabasco sauce (to taste)**
2	**cloves garlic (finely chopped)**
2	**t. lemon juice**
7	**strips bacon (crisp fried and chopped)**
24	**raw oysters in shell**
1	**lb. rock salt**

1. Preheat broiler.
2. Combine all ingredients, except oysters and salt, and set aside.
3. Pour rock salt in shallow oven proof pan.
4. Shuck* oysters. Set oysters in half shells. Place shells on rock salt.
5. Place under broiler until oysters are just warm through.
6. Remove from broiler and top with Kilpatrick Sauce.
7. Broil until sauce is slightly cooked. Serve hot.

Serves: 4
Preparation: 20 minutes

* See Glossary under Shuck for directions.

A great way to serve oysters on half shell!

RED SNAPPER LOUISIANE

A LA - La Louisiane

2	lbs. red snapper fillets (cut in 4 portions)
1	egg (beaten)
½	cup milk
2	T. melted butter
	salt and pepper
½	cup flour
½	cup oil
3	T. butter
8	artichoke hearts
4	mushrooms (sliced)
1	t. Worcestershire sauce
1	t. lemon juice
1	t. tarragon vinegar
½	cup sliced almonds (toasted)
4	lemon wedges (garnish)
	parsley (garnish)

1. Beat together egg, milk and melted butter; salt and pepper to taste.
2. Dip fillet portions in batter, then flour lightly.
3. Heat oil in large frying pan; saute fish until they flake easily with a fork and are lightly brown, about 5 minutes each side.
4. In another skillet, melt butter and saute artichoke hearts and mushrooms. Add Worcestershire sauce, lemon juice and tarragon vinegar. Cook vegetables until tender.
5. To serve, place fillets on serving platter, spoon over artichoke and mushroom sauce and sprinkle with almonds. Garnish with lemon wedges and parsley.

Serves: 4
Preparation: 20 minutes

This is a very easy dish and very elegant to serve.

120

CHICKEN SAUTE

A LA - La Louisiane

2	whole chicken breasts (boned and split)
4	chicken legs (boned)
½	cup flour
½	cup butter
¼	lb. wild rice
2	T. butter
12	artichoke hearts (fresh or canned)
12	fresh mushrooms (sliced)
⅛	cup sherry
1	t. lemon juice
¼	cup Escoffier sauce or good packaged meat gravy

1. Dip chicken pieces lightly in flour.
2. Melt butter in frying pan. Saute chicken in butter in covered frying pan until done, about 20 - 30 minutes.
3. Prepare wild rice according to package directions.
4. In separate pan, melt remaining butter and add artichoke hearts, mushroom slices, sherry, lemon juice and sauce or packaged gravy.
5. Cook until artichoke and mushrooms are done and ingredients are well blended.
6. To serve, place wild rice in bottom of serving dish. Add cooked chicken and spoon artichoke-mushroom sauce over all.

Serves: 4 generously
Preparation: 1 hour

A good flavor combination!

CARAMEL CUSTARD
(Make several hours ahead)

═══════════════════════════════════

A LA - La Louisiane

½	cup sugar
¼	cup water
	pinch of cream of tartar
2	cups milk
1	t. vanilla
3	eggs
2	egg yolks
¼	cup sugar

1. Combine sugar and water in small heavy sauce pan. Bring to boil over high heat, stirring constantly.
2. Stir in cream of tartar. Boil syrup over moderate heat, tipping pan from side to side constantly until syrup turns golden brown. (Will take at least 10 minutes.)
3. Remove from heat and pour slowly into shallow 1 qt. metal or porcelain mold or six individual custard dishes. Coat bottom and sides evenly.
4. Preheat oven to 325°.
5. In a 1½ qt. saucepan, bring milk to frothy stage over medium heat.
6. Remove pan from stove; add vanilla. Set aside.
7. In bowl, beat eggs and egg yolks together with ¼ cup sugar until well mixed and slightly thickened.
8. Stirring constantly, add milk in a thin stream.
9. Strain through a fine sieve into caramel lined mold or individual dishes.
10. Place mold in large pan on middle shelf in oven.
11. Pour enough boiling water into pan to come halfway up sides of mold.
12. Bake custard for one hour or until knife inserted in middle comes out clean. Lower oven temperature if water simmers.

— Continued —

13. Remove mold from water, refrigerate at least 3 hours.
14. To serve: Unmold by running sharp knife around sides and dip bottom of mold in hot water for a few seconds. Place chilled serving plate over mold and quickly invert. Rap plate gently on counter and custard will slide out.
15. Serve cold.

Serves: 6
Preparation: 20 minutes
Refrigerate: 3 hours

Chef suggests that you pour a favorite liqueur over top when serving, for a special flavor!

J. SNITILY 86 ©

Located in the heart of downtown San Antonio, along the Paseo del Rio, Las Canarias is very confortable in La Mansion del Rio Hotel. The oldest section of the hotel was built in 1852 and served as Old St. Mary's School of Law until 1966. Shortly thereafter, the limestone building was converted into a hotel, restored and enlarged. In 1985 the restaurant and hotel underwent another major restoration to their original old elegance and charm. The hotel is a designated Texas Historical Site and in the past has earned awards from the Texas Historical Commission and the San Antonio Conservative Society.

One of the less than fifty worldwide members of the prestigious Preferred Hotel Association, La Mansion del Rio, in addition to award-winning architecture, offers excellent cuisine and a diligent staff. This is best evidenced in Las Canarias.

The restaurant is named in honor of the pioneer family from the Canary Islands, who in 1731 established the first civil settlement in San Antonio. Las Canarias is a first-class interpretation of Spanish architecture and decor in addition to having excellent food.

— Continued —

125

The cuisine is now Southwest-American with a daily changing menu. The former menu featured Spanish fare and those are the recipes that we've included in this printing. The paella is substantial with ample amounts of lobster, oysters, chicken, sausage and green peppers. It will delight you.

The dining room seats 70 plus 22 comfortably in the private dining section. Las Canarias, if not the only, is one of the few restaurants on the river to feature a cruvinet, offering a selection of wines by the glass. To enhance the evening, you'll dine to Classical-Spanish guitar music.

Las Canarias is located at 112 College St. in San Antonio.

MEDITERRANEAN SALAD

A LA - Las Canarias

3	heads bibb lettuce
12	oz. shrimp *(cooked, peeled, deveined, chilled)
1	lemon cut in 6 wedges
12	black olives
6	cherry tomatoes
12	oz. vinaigrette dressing (favorite recipe, bottled oil and vinegar, or see index)

1. Arrange large outside leaves on six chilled plates. Evenly divide remaining lettuce.
2. Place two ounces of shrimp on each plate.
3. Garnish with lemon wedges, olives and cherry tomato.
4. Pour dressing over salad.

Serves: 6
Preparation: 10 minutes

*Chef recommends Titi shrimp. Test kitchen used medium sized shrimp.

A most colorful, good tasting combination.

PAELLA LEVANTINA
Rice with Shellfish and Chicken

━━━━━━━━━━━━━━━━━━━━━━━━━━━━
━━━━━━━━━━━━━━━━━━━━━━━━━━━━

A LA - Las Canarias

2	T. olive oil
½	cup pork tenderloin (cubed)
1	large onion (sliced)
2	green peppers (sliced)
1	tomato (diced)
1	clove garlic
	salt and pepper (to taste)
1½	chickens (quartered) 6 pieces
	oil
3	cups rice
5	cups chicken stock
	pinch of saffron
3	small lobster tails (halved)
12	shrimp
12	clams
12	slices sausage
1	cup green peas (cooked)

1. Preheat oven to 350°.
2. Saute pork in hot oil. Add onion and green peppers. Cook for three minutes.
3. Add tomato, garlic, salt and pepper. Remove from heat.
4. Saute chicken pieces in oil until brown.
5. Combine rice and stock in paella pan or large shallow pan. Mix well.
6. Add all other ingredients (except green peas) including pork mixture and chicken.

— Continued —

7.   Bring to boil over moderate heat.
8.   Cover and bake 20 minutes.
9.   Garnish with hot green peas.

Serves: 6
Preparation: 45 minutes
Cooking time: 20 minutes

A delicious version of this traditional Spanish dish.

CREPES AUX CHOCOLATE

(Begin this three part dessert 1 day ahead or a minimum of 5 hours because of freezing time.)

═══════════════════════════════════

A LA - Las Canarias

¼	cup cocoa
¾	cup flour
1	t. sugar
3	eggs (beaten)
1¾	cups milk
2	t. butter (melted)
¼	cup oil or less to grease crepe pan
	Chocolate Mint Mousse (recipe page 132)
	Vanilla Custard Sauce (recipe page 133)
	Mint leaves (optional) garnish

1. Combine dry ingredients. Stir to mix well.
2. Combine eggs and milk; add slowly to dry ingredients, stirring until smooth.
3. Add melted butter; mix well.
5. Heat crepe pan over moderately high heat and brush lightly with oil.
6. Pour in scant one quarter cup batter and tilt pan quickly to spread batter. Cook for one minute approximately.
7. When done, flip to other side and continue cooking.
8. Slide onto plate and cook remaining batter. Cover crepes with damp cloth and set aside.
9. Next, make Chocolate Mousse on page 132. Fill crepes with mousse; roll and freeze. Since this yields 16 crepes you can use only what you need and keep the others frozen for future desserts.
10. Finally, make Custard Sauce, page 133, and pour hot sauce over filled frozen crepes. Garnish with mint leaves and serve.

— Continued —

Yields: 16 crepes
Preparation: 30 minutes - Crepes
                  30 Minutes - Mousse
                  30 Minutes - Custard Sauce
Freezing: 2 - 3 hours

Delicious with Chocolate Mousse piped down center and warm Vanilla Custard Sauce topping. Use your imagination for other great combinations.

CHOCOLATE MINT MOUSSE

A LA - Las Canarias

2½	cups whipping cream
7	oz. bittersweet chocolate
4	T. water
1	cup sugar
6	T. Creme de Menthe
16	crepes (recipe page 130) optional – see note below

Vanilla Custard Sauce (recipe page 133) optional – see note below

1. Whip cream until peaks form. Set aside.
2. Over low heat melt chocolate with water. Stir until smooth.
3. Add sugar and Creme de Menthe.
4. Bring to a boil, then cool.
5. Fold into whipped cream. You may use as is or go on to next step.
6. Pipe mousse down center of chocolate crepes and roll up. Freeze for 2-3 hours.
7. Next, make Vanilla Custard Sauce. Recipe on page 133.

Yields: 3 cups filling
Preparation: 30 minutes

A delicious mousse. Serve as filling for crepes (page 130) topped with Vanilla Custard Sauce (page 133); or use in pie crust and tart shells; or finish with step 5, put into dessert glasses and chill.

VANILLA CUSTARD SAUCE

A LA - Las Canarias

2	**cups milk**
3	**T. sugar**
6	**eggs**
½	**t. vanilla**

1. Heat milk and add sugar. Cook and stir until just dissolved. Do not boil.
2. Beat eggs and pour heated milk over eggs while stirring constantly.
3. Place in double boiler and cook over hot water. Do not let milk boil.
4. Cook until sauce coats the spoon.
5. Add vanilla and chill (unless you are using it immediately).
6. Reheat and serve over Chocolate Crepes, page 130.

Yield: 2 cups
Preparation: 30 minutes

This is also good over fresh berries and fruit pies!

J. SNITILY 86 ©

La Reserve is situated within the fashionable Inn on the Park Hotel which resides on a twenty-eight acre park at Four Riverway in the Galleria area of Houston. A full range of amenities are available including several large swimming pools, tennis courts and jogging paths.

The hotel's lobby houses The Palm Court which dispenses afternoon tea, evening cocktails, hors d'oeuvres and the consonant notes of a piano in capable hands. At one end, beyond the flower boxes and open French doors, is Le Bar, which provides comfortable seating, handsome furnishings and an elaborate array of liqueurs and eaux-de-vie. Le Bar lies but several steps from La Reserve and the heart of the matter.

La Reserve is a genteel room, with brown patterned carpeting, finely grained tables and dark-wooded walls. Small lamps anoint each table's elegant setting. Delicate pink and violet floral patterns grace the china and lose little face alongside live counterparts sitting adjacent the scalloped, silver butter tray. Table linens are starched and sharply creased, while the napery is silken soft.

— Continued —

135

Maitre d' Serge Rondelez is devoted to carrying out his mission of servicing La Reserve's patrons in an uncompromising and gracious manner.

Serge introduced an appetizer of Pheasant Mousse and explained the preparation of its blueberry vinegar sauce, which is the end product of a lengthy reduction process rather than the use of thickeners. Very rich, I ingested the whole over several pieces of toast.

An entree of Lamb Medallions, overlapped in circular fashion atop a bed of blanched spinach and mushrooms was an exquisite affair. Lean, tender, entirely delicious and served in a fashion unique to Texas, the presentation wears well within these walls.

Cheese can offer a respite from visually sophisticated offerings and yet continue to provide the diner an education in varied tastes within a given medium. La Reserve has a fine selection of cheeses and will forever be remembered as having introduced me to St. Andre. Smooth, buttery and mild, this triple cream cheese deserves your acquaintance and will certainly dispense its many blessings upon your palate.

La Reserve respects fruit sherbets for their light and refreshing contrast to the aforementioned heavy-weights. I was introduced to their rewards in triplicate. Trois-Sorbet was a plate of youthful color with spherical offerings of strawberry, apricot and raspberry, each nestled in a puree of the other. Strawberries, raspberries and mint leaves provided the garnish. Alone, the Trois-Sorbet lends credibility to the concept of Nouvelle Cuisine, evidencing a unique identity and direction.

At the dinner hour, Le Grand Menu, or "Degustation" offers a unique opportunity to sample six entrees, each individually presented and several desserts.

The luncheon menu offers an economical look into the talents of this fine restaurant. The three course, prix fixe meal includes soup, an entree, dessert and coffee.

— Continued —

Finally, Serge left no doubts that there is a total willingness to prepare special menues to meet the wishes of individual diners. In fact, a Four Seasons Hotel Alternative Menu features items that are low in sodium, cholesterol and calories (550 calories for a two-course lunch and 650 for a three-course dinner). Through his devotion and more than twenty years to refine his skills, Serge Rondelez has molded his responsibilities into a state of art whose renderings are the framework of each patron's meal.

La Reserve is located at Four Riverway in Houston.

CHILLED PHEASANT MOUSSE WITH BLUEBERRY VINEGAR SAUCE

A LA - La Reserve

1	Pheasant, 16 - 20 oz.
2	T. pate de foie gras (available in grocery gourmet section)
3	T. butter
2	T. brandy
1	T. Pommery seed mustard or coarse grain mustard salt and white pepper (to taste)
¾ - 1	cup whipping cream (whipped to soft peaks)

— Blueberry Vinegar Sauce —

1	cup red wine vinegar
¾	t. whole black pepper (crushed)
¼	cup sugar
1	T. raspberry jelly with seeds
¼	cup fresh or frozen blueberries
½	lemon (zested) *
	melba toast or other toast (optional accompaniment)

1. Preheat oven to 350°
2. Tie, season with salt and pepper and roast pheasant for 15 minutes or until done.
3. Cool. Remove skin, bones, tendons and tough tissue from meat and discard. Chill pheasant in freezer for 10 minutes.
4. Run meat, pate and butter through small hole grinder, two times, or process in food processor until finely ground.
5. Season with brandy, mustard, salt and pepper.
6. Fold meat into whipped cream. Chill in freezer while making the sauce.

— Continued —

══

— **Blueberry Vinegar Sauce** —

7.   Place wine vinegar, black pepper and sugar in stainless steel pan over medium high heat and cook until reduced by half, approximately 10-15 minutes. Remove from stove and let cool.
8.   While cooling, whisk in jelly. Add blueberries. Let cool in refrigerator while you shape mousse into quenelles.
9.   With large tablespoon, scoop up pheasant cream mixture and shape into oblong, slightly rounded quenelles**
10.   Place quenelles on chilled plates. Pour blueberry vinegar sauce over and around quenelles. Garnish with thin strips of lemon zest.
11.   Serve with melba toast as an appetizer.

Serves: 4
Preparation time: 60 minutes

* Lemon zest is the grated peeling from the lemon rind. Avoid the white portion under the rind as it's bitter.
**The classic quenelle egg shape is best achieved by using a second tablespoon turned upside down to pat the mound into a nice rounder shape.

An elegant appetizer for a very special occasion.

LOBSTER MOUSSE WITH CAVIAR BUTTER SAUCE

A LA - La Reserve

— Mousse —

½	lb. uncooked lobster meat (reserve shells)
1	cup heavy cream (whipping)
	salt and pepper (to taste)
2	T. brandy
¼	cup white wine
2	T. shallots (finely chopped)

— Timbales —

4	timbale molds or pyrex custard dishes
¼	cup butter (room temperature)
1	large or 2 medium turnips (peeled)
4	large carrots (peeled)
1	lobster tail (cooked and sliced into 4 medallions – reserve shells)
¼	cup Beluga Caviar or other brand

— Sauce —

¼	cup olive oil
	reserved shells
¼	cup celery (finely diced)
½	cup leeks (washed and finely diced)
1	sprig tarragon or ¼ t. dry
1	sprig thyme or ¼ t. dry
½	t. white pepper
1	bay leaf
4	sprigs parsley
¼	cup brandy
1	cup fish stock or broth (can be made by poaching one of the shells in 1 cup water for 3 minutes - strain)
1	cup white wine
1	t. tomato paste
1	cup whipping cream

— Continued —

— Mousse —

1.   To make mousse, combine lobster meat, heavy cream, salt, pepper, brandy, white wine and shallots in food processor bowl. Process until blended and smooth, approximately 2-3 minutes. Set mousse aside.

— Timbales —

2.   Butter molds or custard dishes.
3.   Thinly slice turnips and carrots. Cut to fit the length of molds and ½" wide.
4.   Drop slices in boiling water for 1 - 2 minutes to blanch. Next, immerse immediately in ice water.
5.   Line molds with alternate layers of carrots and turnips.
6.   Top with mousse to fill half way. Place lobster medallion on top. Divide caviar equally between four molds and place in center of medallion. Top with additional mousse. Tap down lightly on hard surface to remove air pockets. Preheat oven to 275°.
7.   Place timbales in large shallow pan. Pour boiling water into pan.
8.   Cover timbales with buttered parchment paper and bake for 25 minutes or until inserted knife comes out clean. Keep hot.

— Sauce —

9.   In large sauce pan saute shells in olive oil for several minutes. Add celery, leeks, herbs and spices. Saute additional 5 - 8 minutes.
10. Flame* with brandy; add fish stock, white wine and tomato paste. Let sauce cook over low heat to reduce by half, approximately 15 - 20 minutes.
11. Next, add cream. Stir and cook until reduced by half, approximately 15 minutes. Pass sauce through a fine sieve or cheese cloth.

— Continued —

12. Unmold cooked timbales onto warm plates. Pour sauce around timbales and serve.

Serves: 4 for 1st course
Preparation time: 60 - 70 minutes

* See Glossary on how to "flambe"

A unique appetizer!

POTATO SAUSAGE WITH CAVIAR
Saucisson Chad De Pomme De Terre Et Caviar

A LA - La Reserve

2	lbs. potatoes (peeled)
1	egg white
¼	cup parsley (minced)
2	hard cooked eggs (peeled and minced)
	salt (to taste)
2-3	yards hog casing (soaked in water) * (read below where this is optional)
2-3	yards butcher twine *
½	cup butter
½	cup caviar
½	cup sour cream

1. Preheat Oven to 250°.
2. Cook potatoes in boiling, salted water until tender. Dry in oven to remove moisture.
3. Rub through sieve or mash with fork. Add egg white, parsley, hard cooked eggs and salt. Mix together.
*4. Run water through casing to check for holes.
*5. Fill a large pastry bag with nozzle with potato mixture. Thread all casing over nozzle. Slowly force mixture into casing. Tie every six inches.
*6. Poach sausages in simmering water for 4 - 6 minutes. Remove and drain.
7. In fry pan, saute pancakes * or sausages in butter until golden brown.
8. Serve with sour cream and caviar.

Serves: 4
Preparation: 1 hour, 45 minutes
Quick method: 1 hour total (includes boiling potatoes)

* Optional! To make a quicker version, skip steps 4, 5 and 6. Shape potato mixture into pancakes and saute in butter. (Test kitchen).

NAPOLEON OF SALMON

A LA - La Reserve

— Lobster Sauce —

2	lbs. lobster shells or small section of lobster *
½	cup olive oil
¼	cup carrots (finely diced)
¼	cup celery (finely diced)
½	cup white parts of leeks (finely chopped)
1	sprig fresh tarragon or 1 t. dried
1	sprig fresh thyme or 1 t. dried
½	t. white pepper
1	bay leaf
4	sprigs parsley
¼	t. cayenne pepper
¼	cup cognac
1	cup fish stock or clam nectar (canned or fresh)
1	cup white wine
1	T. tomato paste
2	qts. whipping cream
	salt and pepper (to taste)

— Napoleon of Salmon —

1	lb. puff pastry (buy in bakery or frozen foods section)
	parchment paper
2½	lbs. spinach (cleaned)
2	t. clarified butter **
½	cup shallots (finely chopped)
1	lb. mushrooms (sliced)
	clarified butter ** (to saute salmon)
2½	lbs. salmon filets (thinly sliced in 2 oz. medallions)
	salt and pepper (to taste)

— Continued —

— Lobster Sauce —

1. Saute lobster shells in large heavy stockpot in olive oil for 4 - 6 minutes.
2. Add vegetables, herbs and spices. Saute for 5 - 8 minutes.
3. Flame with cognac. ***
4. After flames die down, add fish stock, white wine and tomato paste. Cook until reduced by one half.
5. Add cream; cook and reduce by one half again.
6. Strain through cheese cloth. Season with salt and pepper. Keep hot and set aside.

— Napoleon of Salmon —

1. Preheat oven to 350°.
2. Roll out puff pastry to ⅛" thickness. Place on sheet pan covered with parchment paper. Bake until light brown and puffy (approximately 15 - 20 minutes); cool and slice into 16 - 2" x 4" pieces.
3. Blanch spinach in boiling salted water for 10 seconds. Shock in ice water to retain color. Remove from water. Dry between 2 towels.
4. In saucepan place 1 teaspoon clarified butter and half of the shallots. Cook over medium heat for 30 seconds.
5. Add spinach and saute. Remove and keep warm.
6. Place one teaspoon clarified butter, remaining shallots and mushrooms in another pan. Saute mushrooms. Remove and keep warm.
7. In a teflon pan, heat butter and saute salmon medallions, until they flake easily with fork.
8. To assemble, place layer of pastry on plate. Next, place a layer each of: mushrooms, spinach and salmon; top with puff pastry. Ladle sauce over and around the napoleon on plate. Do this for eight servings.

— **Continued** —

Serves: 8
Preparation: Sauce - 1 hour
             Napoleon - 30 minutes

* This is just for the lobster flavor. Any section, piece or flavoring of lobster will do.
** See Glossary under Clarified Butter
*** See Glossary if you need information on how to flambe.

A delicious dish! Try it for a special dinner.

le Restaurant de France

Le Restaurant de France, an appellation that allows little lassitute, can seldom be charged with pretentiousness. Located in Houston's Hotel Meridien this repository of Gallic cooking is establishing itself as one of the city's most reliable sources for ambitious interpretations of contemporary French cooking.

Offering both a la carte and fixed price meals, the menu shows creativity and the attendant confidence. For example, the Terrine of Wild Duck with Pickled Vegetables is a rigorous offering for an appetizer. Diners deem this marbled melange of texture, color, and bouquet, an unreserved success.

A partial noting of soups includes Chilled Light Cream of Fresh Asparagus, Seafood Consomme garnished with Whole Oysters, and Hot Cream of Chive with Noilly.

Various salads of mixed green vegetables come dressed in basil-butter. The Lobster Salad is resplendent; intricately assembled and couched in truffle-butter dressing; it is enough to serve two.

The luncheon menu emphasizes lighter seafood entrees, including Fricasseed Bay Scallops with Leeks, Medallions of Monkfish in Peppercorn Sauce, and Filet of Snapper Baked in Creamed Spinach.

— Continued —

Dinner entrees lean to meats, with selections such as Boneless Veal Tenderloin served in a delicate calvados sauce with sauteed apples. Beef Tenderloin in Paprika Sauce may remind one of Louisiane cayenne.

Desserts more than hold their own. The Thinly Sliced Apples in Pastry and Rich Ceam; Pear and Almond Tortes; and Chocolate Mousse Cakes cause the pastry trolley to stop at many a table.

For those of you who stiffen at the thought of entering a fashionable French restaurant, let the luncheon menu allay your fears and the experience lighten your heart.

Le Restaurant de France is located at 400 Dallas in Houston.

MIGNONS DE VEAU AUX POMMES
Veal with Cognac Cream Sauce

A LA - Le Restaurant De France

2	large apples (peeled)
¼	cup butter
½	cup sugar
¼	cup butter (to saute)
4	6 oz. filets of veal loin (salted and peppered)
1	lemon (peeled and thinly sliced)
3	T. Calvados or apple brandy
3	T. cognac
1	qt. whipping cream

1. Preheat oven to 350°.
2. Slice apples into 6 pieces each.
3. In a heavy frying pan melt butter; add sugar and apple slices. Saute until apples are light brown on all sides. Place apples in preheated oven for 5 minutes.
4. In a separate pan, melt ¼ cup butter and lightly fry the veal loins with slices of lemon for 3 - 5 minutes on each side. Cook for 2 more minutes and remove meat from pan and keep warm.
5. In same pan with lemon slices, add Calvados and cognac and deglaze * by scraping and stirring while cooking over low heat.
6. Add cream. Continue cooking and stirring the sauce until reduced by half, approximately 10 minutes.
7. Strain sauce through fine strainer; keep warm.
8. Arrange veal and apple slices on plate.
9. Pour sauce over both and serve immediately.

Serves: 4
Preparation: 30 minutes

* See Glossary if you need more information on "Deglaze".

A refreshing combination!

149

L'EMINCE DE QUEUES DE HOMARD
Lobster Tail Salad

═══════════════════════════════════

A LA - Le Restaurant De France

4	medium lobster tails
4	artichoke hearts (canned)
6	large white mushrooms
2	fresh tomatoes
2	small hearts red leaf lettuce (separated, washed and dried)
½	T. lemon juice
5	T. white wine
¾	lb. butter (cut in walnut size pieces)
½	T. wine vinegar
	salt and pepper (to taste)
¼	t. mustard
6	T. walnut oil

1. Preheat oven to warm.
2. Cook lobster tails in boiling water for 15 minutes or until done. Remove from water and carefully lift tail out of shell. Do not overcook!
3. Slice tail meat lengthwise, as thinly as possible.
4. Thinly slice artichoke hearts and mushrooms. Set aside.
5. Peel and dice tomatoes and set aside.
6. Tear lettuce into bite size pieces and set aside.
7. Combine lemon juice and wine in heavy saucepan. Reduce by one half over medium high heat.
8. Remove pan from heat. Whisking continuously, add two pieces of butter. As they melt, add butter, one piece at a time and whisk until each is incorporated. If butter starts to congeal, return pan to very low heat or over pilot light. Set aside over pilot light or luke warm water to keep melted until last step.
9. In a separate bowl, make vinaigrette by combining remaining ingredients.

— Continued —

150

10. Pour over torn lettuce leaves and toss. Arrange lettuce in dome shape on individual plates.
11. Arrange lobster, mushrooms and artichokes around the lettuce.
12. Place tomatoes in center of lettuce.
13. Put plates in oven for one minute so salad will be served slightly warm. Remove.
14. Drizzle warm butter sauce over plates and serve immediately.

Serves: 4
Preparation: 45 minutes

Scrumptuous fare! Serve as main dish or extraordinary salad.

SUPREME OF DUCK WITH POACHED MANGO

(Begin Early in Day)

═══════════════════════════════════

A LA - Le Restaurant De France

2	large ducks (about 5 - 6 lbs. each)
¼	cup oil
3	carrots (cut in small pieces)
2	onions (cut in small pieces)
2	cups white wine
	salt and pepper (to taste)
6	juniper berries (optional)
3	mangos
2	cups white wine
⅛	t. sugar
	salt and pepper
1	qt. heavy whipping cream

1. Preheat oven to 350°.
2. Remove neck and giblets from duck cavities. Place them in saucepan and add only enough water to cover. Simmer until tender. Set aside. (Do not discard liquid).
3. Salt and pepper inside of duck cavities and place in roasting pan in oven.
4. Roast until done, approximately 1½ - 2 hours or 20 minutes per pound.
5. Remove meat from bones. Set meat aside. Save roasting juices.
6. Cut or break bones into pieces.
7. In frying pan with oil, fry bones and carrots and onions. Cook until bones are brown.
8. Add 2 cups white wine and cook until reduced by three quarters. Set aside.
9. Remove neck and giblets from cooking liquid and discard. Combine cooking liquid and juices from roasting pan. Cool and remove fat.

— Continued —

10. Add juices to bones; season with salt and pepper and add berries.
11. Continue cooking until reduced to desired sauce thickness. Strain through a fine strainer and set aside.
12. Peel mangos. Slice in half and remove seed, keeping fruit intact as much as possible. Place in separate pot.
13. Cover with white wine, seasoned with sugar, salt and pepper. Poach until done. Knife will pierce mangos smoothly when done. Remove mangos from liquid. Save liquid and fruit.
14. Take half the liquid and reduce by cooking on high heat until only a few teaspoons remain. (Discard remaining liquid).
15. Add quart of heavy cream and reduce three quarters of it by simmering slowly, about 30 minutes. Stir often. Don't burn.
16. Add the reserved liquids from Step 11 and boil until well reduced. The cream will turn a light caramel color and cover smoothly the back of a spoon. This will take about 20 minutes.
17. Pass the sauce through a strainer and keep warm.
18. Slice duck meat thinly and reheat. Slice mangos without going all the way through one end, so that it will fan out. Reheat.
19. Arrange three - four slices of meat on plate and fan of mango.
20. Place plates in oven to rewarm. Cover meat with sauce, but do not cover the mango.
21. Serve immediately.

Serves: 6
Preparation: 4 hours including roasting time.

This is a delicious dish well worth the extra effort. Can be done in stages to simplify.

FEVILLETE AUX REINETTES
Puff Pastry with Apples

A LA - Le Restaurant De France

1   sheet puff pastry - 10 inches across (buy in bakery or frozen food section)
2   green apples (peeled)
¼-½   cup sugar (to taste)
1   cup whipped cream

1.   Preheat oven to 400°.
2.   Arrange the puff pastry on a baking sheet.
3.   Slice the apples very thinly and arrange on top of puff pastry.
4.   Sprinkle with sugar.
5.   Bake in oven for 15 minutes or until pastry puffs and turns golden.
6.   Serve either warm or at room temperature topped with whipped cream.

Serves: 4 - 6
Preparation: 10 minutes
Baking time: 15 minutes

A very simple light dessert. Perfect after a heavy meal or for mid-morning coffee or afternoon tea.

the Mansion on Turtle Creek

The internationally famous Mansion on Turtle Creek represents different things to different people. To land developers, the Mansion represents four-and-one half acres of formerly under-utilized prime location which uses the original building as the theme and alongside it developed a luxurious hotel. To persons ruled by history, pre-contemporary artistic leanings and refined gustatory inclinations, the Spanish-styled, Sheppard King Mansion represents a better life, a glimpse of Texas' romantic past and meals that still evidence man's capacity for creating vestiges of genteel living.

Located five minutes from Dallas' central business district, the restored Sheppard King Mansion is a stuccoed, three-storied estate of Spanish Alhambra inspiration.

From the courtyard, a canopied entrance leads to a rotunda foyer with a grand staircase, marble flooring, paintings and a large antique bronze chandelier.

The main dining room boasts two fireplaces, quality art and antiques.

The bar and lounge area features a dark wooden floor, a low beamed ceiling and dark green fabric walls clad with litho-graphs and eighteenth century paintings depicting various hunting scenes.

The eclectic cuisine evidences no less elegance or attention to detail. Appetizers include Beluga Caviar Malossol, Smoked Scottish Salmon and Asparagus Consomme. Following the appetizer, one may attend to the Symphony of Vegetable Mousse or the Cold Lobster on Lamb Lettuce. Entrees seem no less appealing and feature Veal Chops with Calvados Brandy and the Duckling with Blueberries.

For those larks who relish breakfast, the Promenade is a beautiful setting, overlooking the landscaped courtyard, in which to enjoy your morning fare. Mansion on Turtle Creek is located at 2821 Turtle Creek Blvd. in Dallas.

COLD LOBSTER ON LAMB LETTUCE
WITH ROQUEFORT AND BEET SAUCE
(Begin at least 2 hours in advance)

A LA - Mansion on Turtle Creek

2	quarts water
1	bay leaf
¼	cup carrots (chopped)
¼	cup celery (chopped)
1	small onion (sliced)
1	lemon (sliced)
1	t. salt
2	sprigs parsley
4	medium lobster tails
2	cups water
½	lemon (juiced)
2	medium beets (peeled, raw)
	salt and pepper
1	T. sugar
½	T. lemon juice
½	cup whipping cream
½	T. vinegar
2	T. Roquefort cheese (mashed)
	salt and pepper
4	heads lamb lettuce or bibb lettuce
20	Belgium endive leaves or 20 romaine leaves

1. Combine water, bay, carrot, celery, onion, lemon, salt and parsley to make a court bouillon. Bring to a boil over very high heat.
2. Add lobster and cook 10 minutes. Remove lobster and cool.
3. In small stock pot combine 2 cups water, lemon juice, beets, salt, pepper and sugar. Cook over medium heat until beets are tender (30 - 60 minutes). Remove beets and refrigerate them for two hours.

— Continued —

4.   Remove meat from lobster shells. Refrigerate meat.
5.   Dice beets and combine with lemon juice, cream, vinegar and cheese. Mix well; salt and pepper to taste and cool. This is the sauce.
6.   To serve, place lamb lettuce in center of cold plate. Surround with 5 endive leaves. Slice lobster meat; place on top of lettuce, in a circle.
7.   Pour one tablespoon of sauce over lobster. Put remaining sauce in lobster heads (or serving bowl) and place on side. *

Serves: 4
Preparation: 1 hour

* If you have a whole lobster, you can garnish top of salad with claws and serve sauce in lobster head, as they do at The Mansion on Turtle Creek.

A very elegant salad. The colors are superb!

SYMPHONY OF VEGETABLE MOUSSE
(Begin Several Hours Ahead)

A LA - Mansion On Turtle Creek

1	cup peeled carrots (sliced)
1	cup cauliflower
1	cup peeled beets (cooked)
1	cup spinach (no stems)
1	cup broccoli
2	cups whipping cream
5	eggs
1	large boneless chicken breast uncooked (divided in 5 equal portions)
	salt and white pepper

1. Place each vegetable in a separate saucepan.
2. Pour three ounces of cream over each.
3. Cook vegetables over medium heat until cream is reduced by one half. Stir to avoid sticking.
4. Remove from heat and cool to room temperature.
5. In a processor, process each vegetable separately with 1 egg and 1 portion of the breast. Salt and pepper to taste. Keep vegetables separate; refrigerate 2 hours.
6. Preheat oven to 350°. Line inside of 2½ - 3 qt. terrine mold with wax paper and butter lightly.
7. With a pastry bag pipe each vegetable into mold in layers. Start with beets, broccoli, carrots, cauliflower and spinach. Cover with sheet of wax paper.
8. Place terrine mold in pan and add water. Bake for 1 hour.
9. Test with toothpick for doneness. If toothpick is moist, bake for ten to fifteen minutes longer.
10. Remove from oven; cool to room temperature.
11. To serve, remove top wax paper, invert on plate, remove paper. Slice and serve on hot plate.

Serves: 8
Preparation: 1 hour
Baking: 1 hour

Delicious as a cold entree next day. A beautiful dish!

A forty year tradition of superb cuisine, individualized service and elegant decor earmarks this Dallas landmark in fine dining.

Owned and operated by restaurateur Philip J. Vaccaro, Mario's features the finest Northern Italian and Continental cuisine. Many of the house specialties are the original recipes brought to Dallas by the restaurateur's Uncle Mario and Aunt Christine who founded the restaurant in 1943. Mario moved the successful restaurant to its second location shortly before his death in 1958. Today, his wife Christine, still the "ambassador" of Mario's which is now in its fourth location, greets many of the restaurant's original patrons as well as their descendents and newcomers alike continuing a family tradition of caring and individuality.

The menu features a variety of antipasti and entrees of pasta, fish, chicken, veal and beef dishes. Time-tested favorites include Fettucine Alfredo with fresh sweet butter, Parmesan cheese and cream; Manicotti alla Siciliana stuffed with homemade ricotta cheese; fresh lemon sole; rack of lamb with garlic as well as breaded cutlet of veal served with fresh tomato sauce and mozarella cheese.

— Continued —

To complete the evening, Mario's offers an array of enchanting desserts including Grand Marnier Mousse, the souffle of the day and Zabaglione.

The ambiance of Mario's reflects the traditional statement of elegance. Rich, red fabric adorns the walls enhancing the shimmer of candlelight. A collection of exquisite Venetian glass is displayed on open shelves which divide the main dining room into two more intimate seating areas. Crystal chandeliers add to the elegance of the dining experience. Reservations are required.

Mario's is located at 135 Turtle Creek Village, Oak Lawn at Blackburn, in Dallas.

GAMBERI MARIO

Shrimp Appetizer

A LA - Mario's

24	**jumbo shrimp (peeled and deveined)**
½	**cup flour**
¼	**cup olive oil**
6	**shallots (finely diced)**
1	**t. garlic (finely diced)**
⅛	**cup parsley (finely chopped)**
½	**cup chicken stock**
2	**T. lemon juice**
½	**cup butter (cut in small chunks)**

1. Dust shrimp with flour.
2. Heat oil over medium high heat. Add shrimp; saute for 2 - 3 minutes until half done.
3. Add shallots. Saute one minute longer until tender.
4. To pan, add garlic, parsley, stock and lemon juice.
5. Cook so that flavors combine and juices reduce down.
6. Slowly add butter chunks while stirring, allowing butter to melt and blend into sauce.
7. Serve immediately.

Serves: 6 as appetizer, 3 or 4 as main dish
Preparation: 15 - 20 minutes

Fresh herbs allow the flavor of shrimp to shine!

GAMBERI ALLA NUOVA-CUCINA

Shrimp Saute with Julienne of Vegetables, Truffles and Lime Juice

A LA - Mario's

4	**T. olive oil**
4	**shallots (minced)**
1	**t. garlic (minced)**
3	**leaves fresh basil or ½ t. dry basil**
1	**carrot (cut julienne) ***
3	**artichoke bottoms (slivered)**
10	**large mushrooms (sliced)**
40	**medium shrimp (peeled, deveined and dredged in flour)**
½	**cup chicken stock**
½	**cup dry white wine**
1	**lime (juiced)**
1	**truffle (cut to julienne) (optional)****
½	**lb. unsalted butter (cut into small pieces)**
	lime zest or lime crown (garnish - optional)***

1. Heat olive oil in saucepan; saute shallots, garlic and basil slowly.
2. When shallots begin to turn transparent, add carrot, artichokes and mushrooms. Saute for 3 minutes.
3. Add shrimp and saute for 3 minutes. Shrimp will be half cooked.
4. Add chicken stock, wine, and lime juice. Simmer for 3 minutes. Add truffle. Do not overcook shrimp.
5. When sauce begins to thicken, stir in butter bit by bit. When all butter has melted, dish is ready to serve.
6. Garnish with strips of lime peel or lime crown. Cool and serve.

— Continued —

Serves: 4
Preparation: 18 minutes

*To cut "julienne" is to cut into thin strips, 1½ inch long by ¼ inch wide.
** An underground fungus that's a food delicacy - Pungent aroma!
***Chef suggests a garnish of julienne of lime zest (peel) or lime crown (lime cut in half, zig zag fashion or tulip cut.)

This is yummy!

FETTUCCINE PASTA

A LA - Mario's

3½	cups flour (sifted)
5	whole eggs
1	T. olive oil
1	t. salt
3	quarts water with 1 T. olive oil and 1 t. salt.
	Sauce Basilico (page 165, or sauce of your choice)

1. Mound flour on a board and scoop out center to form a well.
2. Break eggs into a bowl; beat well with olive oil and salt.
3. Pour egg mixture into flour well.
4. With fingers, mix flour into eggs, a little at a time, until it is well mixed.
5. Knead the mixture with both hands until very firm and smooth to the touch.
6. Dip a clean cloth in warm water. Wring out well. Wrap the dough in the damp cloth. Set aside for one half hour.
7. Roll the dough into paper thin sheets, one foot wide by one foot long.
8. Cut into strips one quarter inch wide. Let rest for five to ten minutes.
9. Fill a four-quart saucepan with three-quarts water. Add olive oil and salt.
10. Bring to a boil and add fettuccine. Stir to prevent fettuccine from sticking together.
11. Bring to a second boil. Cook two minutes.
12. Strain in colander; pour cold water over pasta.
13. Pour Sauce Basilico (next page) or your favorite sauce over the pasta and serve.

Serves: 4
Preparation: 1½ hours.

Fresh noodles for your favorite sauce or festive occasion!
Great with Sauce Basilico, page 165!

SAUCE BASILICO

A LA - Mario's

2	T. olive oil
4	cloves garlic (coarsely sliced)
28	oz. peeled plum tomatoes (broken into pieces)
8 - 10	leaves fresh basil *
	salt and pepper (to taste)
1	cup whipping cream
1	lb. pasta (cooked al dente**) or use Fettuccine Pasta recipe on page 164
¾	cup freshly grated Parmesan cheese***

1. In medium sauce pan, heat olive oil and saute garlic until lightly brown.
2. Add tomatoes and basil. Let simmer until all water and juices have evaporated. Do not burn.
3. Salt and pepper to taste. Add cream and simmer for two minutes.
4. Place pasta in a serving bowl. Top with sauce and mix well. Sprinkle generously with Parmesan.

Serves: 4 - 6
Preparation: 15 minutes

* Chef says it is important to use only fresh basil because of its aroma!
** See Glossary
*** The secret to great Fettuccine is FRESH grated parmesan.

A wonderful dish! Use with Fettucine Pasta on page 164.

COTOLETTA DI VITELLO ALLA MILANESE
Veal Cutlet with Lemon

A LA - Mario's

1½	lbs. veal cutlets (trimmed and pounded thin) to serve 6 people
	salt and pepper (to taste)
½	cup flour
3	eggs (beaten)
1½	cups bread crumbs
½	cup clarified butter *
½	cup freshly grated Parmesan cheese
1	t. fresh garlic puree **
¼	cup parsley (chopped)
3	lemons (cut in half or quartered)

1. Preheat oven to broil.
2. Salt and pepper cutlets. Dip in flour to coat; shake off excess.
3. Dip in egg and then in bread crumbs. Pat each cutlet to make crumbs adhere.
4. Heat clarified butter in large frying pan. Saute cutlets for 2 - 3 minutes on each side until brown.
5. Place on oven proof platter
6. Combine cheese, garlic and parsley. Top each cutlet with mix.
7. Place under broiler for 1 - 2 minutes until cheese is just brown.
8. Serve warm with lemon halves as garnish.

— Continued —

Serves: 6
Preparation: 20 minutes

* See Glossary under Clarified.
* Either puree your own garlic in a food processor or buy already prepared in store in spice section or gourmet section.

An Italian classic! Simple to prepare!

ORATA BELLISSIMA MUGNAIA
Red Snapper with Shrimp, Mushrooms and Lemon-Butter Sauce

A LA - Mario's

3	lbs. red snapper fillets - 6 nice pieces
1	cup flour
3	eggs (beaten)
½	cup clarified butter *
36	medium sized shrimp
1	lb. large white mushrooms (quartered)
3	shallots (chopped)
½	lb. butter
2	lemons (juiced)
½	cup parsley (chopped)
6	fresh basil leaves (garnish - optional)

1. Dip snapper fillets in flour; shake off excess.
2. Dip floured fillets in eggs to coat.
3. In large frying pan heat clarified butter. Saute snapper until lightly browned, approximately 3 - 5 minutes. Turn and brown other side.
4. Remove fillets from pan and pat with linen cloth or paper towel to remove excess grease.
5. Place on platter and keep warm.
6. In same frying pan, saute shrimp, mushrooms and shallots until shrimp are almost done, approximately 8 minutes.
7. Add ½ lb. of butter and cook over medium heat until butter melts and vegetables are tender.
8. Add lemon juice and parsley; gently stir to mix all ingredients.

— Continued —

9.   Place six shrimp over each snapper fillet.
10.   Pour sauce over snapper and serve. (Garnish with fresh basil leaves if you desire.)

Serves: 6
Preparation: 40 minutes

*See Glossary under Clarified

This delicious dish will make any occasion special.

BISTECCA ALLA GRIGLIA O AL FORNO
New York Sirloin topped with Parmesan Butter Glaze

A LA - Mario's

— Butter Glaze —

½	lb. butter (softened)
6	shallots (chopped)
8	cloves garlic
6	fresh basil leaves or ¼ t. dry basil (optional)
¼	cup whipping cream
¼	cup parsley (chopped)
½	cup parmesan cheese
6	New York cut steaks or steaks of your choice

— Butter Glaze —
1. With electric mixer, whip butter for 15 minutes until butter is white.
2. In food processor, puree shallots, garlic and basil.
3. Add puree, whipping cream and parsley to butter. Whip for additional 2 - 3 minutes.
4. Add Parmesan and whip for 1 minute more.
5. Let mixture stand for 10 minutes so flavors will blend.
6. Preheat broiler.
7. Grill steaks until almost done.
8. Spread butter glaze on each steak.
9. Place under broiler until butter melts and turns light brown, approximately 2 - 3 minutes.
10. Serve immediately.

Serves: 6
Preparation: 20 minutes plus grilling time.

Wonderful topping for steaks! Flavors are great together!

170

Michel Restaurant

Situated on Camp Bowie Blvd. in Fort Worth is Michel Restaurant. The cuisine is French and first class.

The owner, Michel Baudouin, is a most personable fellow and younger brother of Jean-Claude Prevot, owner of Jean-Claude in Dallas. Michel immigrated to Texas in 1978, worked in his brother's restaurant for three years and then moved to Fort Worth after he married a young lady from the Fort Worth area. He renovated one of the oldest residences on Camp Bowie to house his operation. In 1983 he introduced the local citizenry to the pleasures of springtime road rallies complete with country buffet, dinner and lodging. In short, Michel has stepped into the Fort Worth community with both feet and has contributed to the city's vitality in a variety of ways.

The restaurant is located in a large, grey three story frame with white trim and brown double doors. The interior is done in grey, white and burgundy. Several dining rooms provide a total seating capacity of approximately sixty. Illuminated old pictures and candles at each table proved a relaxed and romantic setting. A private dining room with balcony is located on the second floor and accommodates sixteen to twenty diners. Across the hall is a small parlor with an adjoining bar and balcony. This area is popular with theatre and opera patrons wishing an aperitif, appetizer or dessert and coffee.

— Continued —

171

Michel has introduced a four course, prix fixe, verbal menu that allows the kitchen more versatility and the ability to avail itself of the freshest ingredients. The meal includes appetizers, sorbet, entree, salad and dessert. Fish, shellfish, fowl, beef, sweetbreads and veal are all utilized in various ways. Everything is homemade, including breads, sorbets and desserts, even the ice cream. There are bisques, gazpacho, Vichysoisse, casseroles, pates, souffles and mousse.

I commenced my dining with an appetizer of poached ocean scallops in a light cream sauce. My notes verify their excellence, soft, not chewy, neither acidic nor biting, just very, very good . . .

As I guided whipped butter over another slice of French bread salad was put before me. Dark lettuce leaves supported chopped bleu cheese, mushrooms, watercress and an oil and vinegar dressing.

A pear sorbet appeared. It was a testament to the advantages of boiling fresh pears, then detailing their character with a dollop of pear brandy during preparation.

As an entree I selected Duck Breasts with Cherries and Brandy. Served medium rare, it was tender, not oily and the sauce was the splendid result of a dedicated reduction process. Snowpeas, cauliflower and carrots rounded out the plate's capacity.

An aromatic chocolate souffle was brought before me. While the oven's heat lingered, a large spoon bearing the freshest whipped cream was placed in its steamy core. It was perfection, a pardonable frolic with excess, an effort that, while fraught with sugar, delivered a level of satisfaction to soften the hardest heart.

The coffee was rich rather than just strong and although excellent unto itself, a receptical of whipped cream won my spoon's attention several times over.

— Continued —

An extensive wine list, including French and domestic, was available, as well as assorted champagnes, sherries, cognacs and armagnacs.

While not emphasized, Michel caters large and small affairs. A recent occasion was a black tie buffet with more than five-hundred guests in attendance.

Michel Restaurant has its own masterpieces and employs a qualified and genial staff to display them before you.

It is located within walking distance of Fort Worth's finest galleries at 3851 Camp Bowie Blvd.

FRAICHE ASPERGES - CHAUDES A L'HUILE DE NOIX
Hot Asparagus Salad

A LA - Michel Restaurant

	water to cook asparagus
½	t. salt
	2 - 3 lemon slices
2	lbs. fresh asparagus (trimmed and peeled) *
¼	cup unsalted butter
4	T. walnut oil
4	T. red wine vinegar
4	T. white wine
1	T. honey
¼	cup unsalted butter
1	cup shelled walnuts (lightly chopped)
	spinach, watercress or greens of choice for garnish.

1. In a large pot, bring water, salt and lemon slices to boil. Cook asparagus just until tender, about 7 - 10 minutes. Drain well and cool quickly.
2. In saute pan combine ¼ cup butter and walnut oil. Heat.
3. Add asparagus and toss lightly.
4. Add vinegar, wine and honey and cook lightly.
5. Add remaining butter and swirl to melt. Add walnuts and remove from heat.
6. Serve warm on a bed of favorite greens. Top with small amount of the sauce.

Serves: 6
Preparation: 20 minutes

* It isn't necessary to peel green asparagus. If it is white asparagus, peel below the head to remove the bitter flavor in the skin.

A super flavor combination for fresh asparagus!

174

FRAICHE COQUILLE ST. JACQUES VERONIQUE
Scallops in Creamy Sauce with Grapes

A LA - Michel Restaurant

1	lb. fresh white seedless grapes
½	cup white wine
½	lb. unsalted butter
	salt and white pepper (to taste)
1	lb. fresh scallops (cleaned)
3	cups whipping cream
¼	cup parsley (chopped)

1. In a blender or processor, puree ½ grapes with 3 T. of wine. Slice remaining grapes in half and set aside.
2. Into a large pot pour pureed grapes and remaining wine; add butter, salt and pepper and bring to a boil.
3. Add scallops and poach 4 minutes, stirring often.
4. Remove scallops and keep warm.
5. Reduce liquid by two thirds by cooking. Add cream.
6. Reduce liquid by cooking until cream bubbles are small, approximately 15 minutes.
7. Return scallops to the pan; add parsley and grapes. Stir lightly and serve.

Serves: 4 (should serve 4; cook may eat it all)
Preparation: 30 minutes

Divine sauce, rich and creamy. I loved it!

J. SNITILY 86©

The Old Warsaw

One of the consistently award-winning Vaccaro restaurants, The Old Warsaw is perhaps Dallas' most prestigious establishment serving classical French cuisine.

The original owners named the restaurant The Old Warsaw to create a feeling of Warsaw, Poland, in pre-war days when the finest restaurants in Warsaw served only classical French cuisine. Today, under the leadership of restaurateur Philip Vaccaro, who purchased the restaurant in 1970, The Old Warsaw continues the old world tradition of elegance, impeccable service and haute cuisine.

Diners feel pampered in the unhurried ambiance complete with strolling violinists and background music from a grand piano. The decor of dimly lit antique crystal chandeliers set the mood for a luxurious dining experience.

The menu features delectable appetizers from Chef de Cuisine Cherif Brahmi, including terrine of duck with truffles, beluga caviar and scampi baked with crab in pernod sauce.

Entrees include European delicacies such as Chateaubriand with Bernaise Sauce; Braised Pheasant garnished with a puree of chestnuts; Salmon in a Beurre Blanc, and New York Strip deglazed with cognac.

Dessert is, in itself, an elegant experience featuring choices of crepes in a fresh orange and lemon sauce flamed with grand marnier or the highly acclaimed white chocolate mousse as well as pastries, souffles or fresh strawberries with cream. A very special finale to dinner at The Old Warsaw is the Flaming Cafe Pierre prepared with precision at table. Reservations are required.

The Old Warsaw is located at Chateau Plaza, 2515 McKinney Avenue.

177

GRATINEE AU BRIE
Brie Soup

A LA - The Old Warsaw

6	**large slices French bread**
1	**bunch green onions (sliced)**
½	**cup leeks (sliced, white part only)**
1½	**cups mushrooms (diced)**
¼	**cup unsalted butter**
2	**oz. sherry, dry**
4	**cups chicken stock**
1	**cup whipping cream**
2	**T. cornstarch**
2	**oz. sherry, dry**
	salt and pepper (to taste)
6	**thin slices Brie cheese**
6	**oven proof soup bowls or crocks**

1. Preheat oven to 400°.
2. Make 6 croutons by cutting bread into shape to fit oven proof soup bowls. Toast and set side.
3. In large pan, saute green onions, leeks and mushrooms in butter for 3 minutes.
4. Deglaze* pan by adding sherry and stirring up particles at bottom.
5. Add chicken stock and bring to a boil.
6. Add cream and boil again.
7. Combine cornstarch and remaining sherry. Add to soup. Add salt and pepper to taste.
8. Pour into individual oven proof crocks. Place Brie on croutons and float on top. Bake in oven until cheese melts.

Serves: 6
Preparation: 20 minutes

* See Glossary

This is a rich tasting soup. Perfect as 1st course or hearty supper for 4.

178

STEAK TARTARE
Seasoned raw ground Steak

A LA - The Old Warsaw

1	egg yolk (beaten)
1½	T. Dijon mustard
2½	T. olive oil
¼	cup onion (chopped)
¼	T. anchovy (chopped)
1	T. capers
1½	T. chopped gherkin dill pickles
1	T. catsup
2	T. parsley leaves (chopped)
	dash of good port wine
	dash of good cognac
	salt and pepper (to taste)
1	lb. raw ground tenderloin (very lean) or ground top round

1. In small bowl, combine egg yolk and mustard. Stir well.
2. Add oil; beat until well mixed. Set aside.
3. In separate large bowl, combine onion, anchovy, capers, gherkins, catsup, parsley, port and cognac.
4. Add egg mixture, salt and pepper to taste, and ground beef. Mix all ingredients well
5. Serve immediately (uncooked, of course) with French fries for a meal or serve in a mound with toast or pumpernickel for appetizer.

Serves: 4
Preparation: 10 minutes

A delicious version of this classic dish. Very well seasoned.

FAISAN, SAUCE GRAND VENEUR

Roast Pheasant in Red Currant Sauce
(can also use Cornish Hens or Chicken)

A LA - The Old Warsaw

2	pheasant, cornish game hens or chickens (2¼ lb. each)
2	T. unsalted butter
1	T. vegetable oil
1	medium onion (diced)
2	small carrots (diced)
6	whole peppercorns (crushed)
1	cup mushrooms (sliced)
2	sprigs parsley (chopped)
1	clove garlic (crushed)
2	T. red wine vinegar
1	cup dry red wine
2	cups veal stock or chicken broth
½	cup whipping cream
4	T. red currant jelly
2	T. cognac or brandy
2	T. unsalted butter (in small pieces)

1. Preheat oven to 350°.
2. Remove wings, neck and giblets from pheasant. Rinse cavities and pat dry.
3. Roast birds in oven until done, approximately one hour.
4. Meanwhile, make sauce by sauteing wings, necks and giblets in butter and oil until golden brown.
5. Add onions, carrots, peppercorns, mushrooms, parsley and garlic. Simmer 4 minutes.
6. Add vinegar, red wine and stock. Reduce to one half by cooking.
7. Add cream and simmer four minutes.
8. Add jelly and simmer two minutes. Remove immediately. DO NOT COOK LONGER.
9. Strain through cheesecloth or fine strainer.

— Continued —

10. Finish sauce by adding cognac. Next add butter, piece by piece, while whisking.
11. Carve pheasants into serving pieces; top with sauce.

Serves: 4
Preparation: 1 hour

This is a great recipe! Delicious on chicken also.

POULET AU MORILLES ET HOMARD

Chicken Breasts Stuffed With Morels, Served With
Medallions Of Lobster

A LA - The Old Warsaw

2	small lobster tails (optional - see footnote)
4	chicken breasts (boned)
1	oz. dry morels (soaked overnight, drained) or 4 oz. mushroom caps (diced)
2	cups chicken stock
1	T. unsalted butter
1	shallot (chopped)
6	large mushrooms (sliced)
1	medium carrot (peeled and cut into fine julienne) *
1	medium leek (trimmed and cut into fine julienne) *
2	cups whipping cream
	salt and pepper (to taste)

1. Steam lobster tails for ten minutes.
2. Remove meat from shells and slice into medallions. Cut in even number to distribute to four plates. Set aside.
3. With a mallet, flatten breasts so they are a uniform thickness.
4. Divide morels into four portions and place in center of each breast.
5. Roll breasts compactly and place seam side down in saucepan. Add chicken stock.
6. Boil gently for fifteen minutes, turning breasts over once.
7. Remove chicken and keep warm. Save stock.
8. Boil stock until reduced to one half. Set aside.
9. In a large pan, melt butter over medium high heat. Add shallots, mushrooms, carrots and leeks. Cook until tender.
10. Slowly stir in reduced chicken stock and cream.
11. Cook until sauce thickens, about ten minutes. Season to taste with salt and pepper.

— Continued —

12. Slice breasts diagonally. Pour some sauce into center of plate and coat evenly. Place sliced breast meat in a circle around plate and arrange lobster in center.
13. Pour remaining sauce over all.

Serves: 4
Preparation: 45 minutes

* To cut "julienne" is to cut into long thin 1½ inch strips, thinner than French fries.

A wonderful combination. If you can't afford lobster, try the chicken and sauce. Chef suggests accompaniments of asparagus and new potatoes.

J. SNITILY 86 ©

This award winning restaurant has quickly taken its place as one of San Antonio's premier dining establishments.

Located on the Paseo del Rio at One Riverwalk Place, P.J.'s is a class operation from location, to appointments, to cuisine.

Seating in the dining room affords an advantageous view of the Riverwalk as well as an appreciation for the talents of interior designer Rosemari Agostine. An effective use of various shades of greens, along with mauve and burgundy, creates variegating dispositions from the resuscitating cooling effect to a warming sensation that evaporates the accumulated tensions of the day. Hand-carved lattice work and original paintings provide relief-of-field and interior focus.

The cuisine, in keeping with the decor, accommodates various inclinations. On balance, aside from the hors d'oeuvres which are largely Gallic, the selections seem evenly distributed between Italian and French cuisine.

— Continued —

Soups include Gazpacho, Minestrone, and the Soup de Fruit de Mer, while broad-leafed salads offer a goat cheese garnish or tuna and potato.

The entrees are not only diverse, but also extensive. The Linguine aux Moules incorporates linguine with cream, mussels and tomato provencal. The salmon is poached in a sauce made with fresh basil, and the Fettuccine al Pesto features homemade fettucine served with pine nuts in a light garlic-flavored sauce. The Red Snapper Shizo presents this delectable denizen steamed, seasoned with soy sauce, and served with sliced vegetables and chives.

P.J.'s will awaken even dormant taste buds to a new day in dining.

P.J.'s is located at One Riverwalk Place on the Paseo del Rio.

SOUPE DE FRUIT DE MER

Seafood Soup

A LA - P.J.'S Restaurant

8	oysters
16	clams
16	mussels
16	medium shrimp (cleaned, peeled and deveined)
¼	cup butter
½	cup leeks (diced)
½	cup celery (diced)
1	cup clam juice *
3	cups water
1	cup potatoes (peeled and diced)
½	cup tomatoes (diced)
	pinch fresh basil or ¼ t. dry basil

1. In a large pot steam oysters, clams,and mussels in about ¼ inch of water for about 6-8 minutes or until done. During last 3 minutes, add shrimp. Do not overcook. Remove from shells and set aside.
2. In a deep saucepan melt butter and saute leeks and celery until soft.
3. Add clam juice, water and potatoes. Cook for ten minutes.
4. Add seafood and tomatoes. Heat until warm.
5. Sprinkle with basil before serving.

Serves: 8
Preparation: 25 minutes.

* You can purchase canned clam juice in grocery store.

A mild flavored seafood soup, seasoned perfectly.

RED SNAPPER SHIZO

A LA - P.J.'S Restaurant

4	6 oz. filets of red snapper
	salt and white pepper (to taste)
4	t. soy sauce
	pinch of celery salt
¼	cup butter
2	leeks - white part (cut julienne) *
1	carrot (cut julienne) *
1	bunch fresh chives (chopped)
¼	cup water

— Beurre Blanc Sauce —

1	shallot (chopped)
¼	cup vinegar
½	lb. butter (cut into small pieces)
	salt and white pepper (to taste)

1. Season snapper with salt and pepper and sprinkle with soy sauce and celery salt.
2. Wrap snapper in foil and cook in a steamer until done, approximately 10-15 minutes. It's done if fish flakes easily with a fork.
3. In saute pan, melt butter and saute julienned vegetables and chives. Add water. Keep warm.

— Beurre Blanc Sauce —

4. In saucepan, over medium heat, combine shallots and vinegar. Cook until reduced to 1 teaspoon of liquid.
5. Remove from heat; gradually whip in pieces of butter until well incorporated. If the sauce gets too cool, return to a very low heat and whisk well.

— Continued —

6.　　　Strain sauce and season with salt and pepper.
7.　　　To serve, cover snapper with julienne of vegetables and
　　　　spoon Beurre Blanc Sauce over entire dish.

Serves: 4
Preparation: 30 minutes

* "Julienne" is to cut into long, thin 1½ strips, thinner than French
fries.

A wonderful combination!

OYSTERS WITH WHITE LEEKS AND BEURRE BLANC SAUCE

A LA - P.J.'S Restaurant

16	oysters (in shell)
6	leeks - white part only (cut julienne) *
½	cup butter

— Beurre Blanc Sauce —

2	shallots (chopped)
¼	cup vinegar
½	lb. butter (cut in small pieces)
	salt and white pepper (to taste)

1. Shuck oysters and set aside; saving sixteen of the nicest looking deep half shells. **
2. Saute leeks in butter and keep warm.
3. In separate pan, heat oysters for a few minutes until hot. Next, replace in their half shells. Cover with leeks and keep warm in the oven.

— Beurre Blanc Sauce —

4. Combine shallots and vinegar in a saucepan over medium heat. Reduce liquid to one teaspoon by cooking.
5. Remove from heat and gradually whip in butter piece by piece. If butter starts to congeal, return pan to very low heat. Do not put over high heat or sauce will separate.
6. Strain sauce and season with salt and pepper.
7. Spoon sauce over oysters and leeks. Serve immediately.

Serves: 4 as appetizers
Preparation: 15 minutes

*Julienne is to cut into thin match stick-like strips.
** For help on how to shuck, see Glossary.

Try this combination for a new way to serve oysters.

190

pyramid

HOTEL
Dallas

The award winning Pyramid Room, in Dallas' Fairmont Hotel, is named for the massive sparkling, inverted pyramid shaped chandelier which hangs from the restaurant's ceiling.

Fashioned from seventy-five hundred pieces of polished, anodized aluminum with twelve hundred fifty glass faces, this six ton, gold colossus is suspended by hundreds of supports.

The adjoining Pyramid Bar is also striking. A three-walled mural, dedicated to the "Beautiful People Of The Sixties", depicts such activities as camel races in Egypt, Kabuki in Japan, bull fighting in Spain, and the Mardi Gras. Another wall supports a huge metal sculpture impregnated with mineral deposits indigenous to the Southwest.

For those who wish to test other than visual senses, an attentive staff is waiting in the dining area prepared to bring you delectable ambrosia.

From the gleaming kitchen an international menu will surely quell hunger pains. Shrimp Rothschild and Sole En Croute will sustain Gallic preferences, while Pheasant Souvaroff can only make travelers from points East feel a sense of home. Maine lobster will cure the wants of a northeasterner, while lamb, veal, and tender young salmon should do well in representing other points of the compass.

An added attraction is the nineteen-foot high, plexiglass wine rack which seemingly hangs in mid-air, ready to dispense its vintage collection.

Whether it be her appetizers, entrees, desserts, or staff, diners soon appreciate why the Pyramid Room has been the benchmark by which other Dallas dining institutions have long been measured.

The Pyramid Room is located at Ross and Akard in the Fairmont Hotel in Dallas.

VEAL BONAPARTE PYRAMID with PEPPER SAUCE

A LA - The Pyramid

16	oz Wisconsin milkfed veal cut into very thin slices
1	t. butter
1	carrot (chopped)
2	celery sticks (chopped)
½	onion (chopped)
¼	lb. beef trimmings*
1	t. crushed black pepper
½	cup brandy
1	cup veal stock or beef bouillon stock
1	cup whipping cream
2	cups mushrooms (finely chopped)
2	shallots or 1 small onion (finely chopped)
2	T. butter
	salt and pepper (to taste)

1. Roast carrot, celery, onion and beef trimmings in 1 t. butter in pan. Sprinkle with black pepper.
2. Add brandy; tip pan and ignite with match until brandy is absorbed.**
3. Pour stock over mixture and add cream. Cook at moderate heat for 30 minutes until sauce is reduced.
4. Meanwhile, squeeze chopped mushrooms through cloth to extract moisture.
5. In a separate pan, saute mushrooms and shallots in butter. Add veal and salt and pepper (to taste) and saute until golden brown, about 3 minutes on each side. Vegetables will be almost dry.
6. Place mushrooms and onions on platter and lay veal strips on the bed of mushrooms. Strain pepper sauce and pour over veal.

— Continued —

Serves: 4
Preparation: 15 minutes
Cooking: 30 minutes

* or use whatever you have to give the sauce a hint of beef flavor.
** See Glossary under Flambe for more instruction if needed.

One of the most delicious sauces you'll ever eat!

CHICKEN BOHEMIENNE

A LA - The Pyramid Room

1	2 lb. chicken (cut into 6 large pieces)
4	T. olive oil
3	T. butter
1	medium onion (chopped)
1	large fresh tomato (chopped)
1	clove garlic
½	t. fennel
½	t. thyme
½	t. salt
½	t. pepper
1	cup white wine
1	T. sweet pimento (chopped)
1	T. tomato puree
1	T. butter
8	pearl onions
1	t. sugar
3	cups cooked rice (optional)

1. Preheat oven to 350°.
2. Saute chicken in olive oil and remove when brown.
3. In separate pan, melt butter. Saute onion, tomato and garlic. Add fennel, thyme, salt, pepper, wine, pimento and tomato puree.
4. Cook sauce 10 minutes and pour over chicken.
5. Bake for 30 minutes at 350° or until chicken is done.
6. Meanwhile, melt butter in separate sauce pan. Add pearl onions and sugar. Cook until sugar dissolves to make a glaze.
7. When chicken is done, place on platter with sauce and pour onion glaze over top. Serve with rice.

Serves: 4
Preparation: 30 minutes
Baking: 30 minutes
A refreshing new taste for chicken!

RAINBOW LODGE

In reflecting upon my weeks in Texas, there is little doubt that one of the most enjoyable meals and pleasant departures from the turmoil of the expressway was at the Rainbow Lodge. Located near Memorial Drive in Houston, the Rainbow Lodge, all but hidden from view, is insulated from the din of traffic and construction. Here a bird's song need not compete with diesel trucks and jackhammers. The few man-made disturbances would likely be a garden hose watering the verdant lawn or clippers grooming the topiaries standing watch over the distant gazebo, flower beds and large shade trees.

This bucolic atmosphere is more fully understood when one realizes that Buffalo Bayou skirts the length of the property on its far side and provides reason for diners frequently sighting raccoons, opossums, armadilloes, squirrels and red-headed woodpeckers. Closer inspection of the bayou might reveal sunning turtles, a Great Egret, a heron or several canoeists.

Bearing all the trappings of an old hunting lodge, this former

— Continued —

private residence has since been enlarged, renovated and redecorated with antiques from across Texas. A set of original Molly Brown chairs, an old player piano, Oriental rugs, numerous hunting trophies, Art-Deco prints and the stenciled tracks of raccoons and opossums on the hardwood floor provide only a glimpse of the visual potpourri.

In addition to its natural endowments and decor, the Rainbow Lodge is justifiably known for its cuisine. The Exective Chef and four sous-chefs take the freshest of foods and turn out soups, breads, salads, entrees and desserts that command a large following despite little advertising.

The soups are made from scratch and may include French Onion, the Seafood Gumbo and Soup du Jour.

Approximately eight luncheon entrees include daily specials. "Trio Broil" features a changing selection of game, seafood and fowl, broiled, baked and poached according to the nature of the dish and served with fresh vegetables.

Dinner entrees are extensive. Nightly specials may include quail or pheasant and venison when in season. A regular item is the Wienerschnitzel. This very tender milk-fed Wisconsin veal is pounded thin, covered with herbal bread crumbs, sauteed in butter and served with fresh mushroom sauce.

Desserts offer fresh fruits with cream and honey, specialty cheesecakes, Walnut Pie and Creme Caramel.

Sunday Brunch may begin with refreshments on the terrace or in the lounge. A variety of egg dishes, homemade biscuits, fruit pancakes, fresh fish and beef dishes may be enjoyed while live music wends its way through the background.

Updated four or five times per year and presided over by the resident sommelier is a selection of over three-hundred wines. Some of the stock is occasionally on display in the private dining room on the third floor.

A staff of almost sixty employees provides a degree of personal and professional service from cloak room to table. Their

— Continued —

relationship with their employer engenders a family-like atmosphere, a refined team effort, very low turnover and consequently a high level of service and customer satisfaction.

Rainbow Lodge is located at #1 Birdsall in Houston.

SEAFOOD GUMBO

A LA - Rainbow Lodge

¼　cup vegetable oil
¾　cup onion (minced)
¼　cup red bell pepper (minced)
¼　cup green bell pepper (minced)
½　cup celery (minced)
¼　cup fresh seeded jalapeno pepper (minced) (or less to taste)
　　salt (to taste)
2　t. gumbo file (or more to taste) (this seasoning can be found in grocery spice section)
2　cups tomato puree (a thick tomato sauce available in your grocers canned food section or use tomato sauce as a substitute)
　　white pepper (to taste)
　　cayenne pepper (to taste)
⅓　lb. scallops
⅓　lb. oysters
⅓　lb. shrimp
⅓　lb. crabmeat
¼　cup brown roux *
½　lb. fresh okra (sliced) (or frozen or canned)
　　water as needed

1. Heat vegetable oil in soup pot. Add minced onion, peppers, celery and jalapeno pepper. Salt liberally. Cook over medium heat until moisture evaporates.
2. When vegetables are tender, add gumbo file to taste. Chef says it should bind the vegetables and turn them brownish green in color.
3. Simmer gently for 3 - 4 minutes. Stir regularly.
4. Add tomato puree and bring gumbo to a slow simmer. Season to taste with white pepper and cayenne. Continue stirring.

— Continued —

5.   In another pan, poach seafood about 5 minutes or until done, in water to cover. Strain seafood and reserve liquid. Refrigerate poached seafood until ready to use.
6.   Add liquid to gumbo.
7.   Thicken gumbo with brown roux. Simmer 30 - 40 minutes, stirring regularly.
8.   Add seafood and okra. Bring to a boil and simmer until served.

Serves: 6
Preparation: 50 minutes
Cooking: 40 minutes

* To make the roux, melt 2 T. butter in a pan. Add 2 T. flour and stir and cook over low heat until the roux is light brown.

A deliciously seasoned version of a Southern classic. Be sure to try it.

GRAND MARNIER CREME CARAMEL
(Begin at least 6 hours before serving to allow for cooling time)

A LA - Rainbow Lodge

— Caramel Syrup —

1	cup sugar
¼	cup water
¼	t. cream of tartar
6	8 oz. souffle cups

— Custard —

2½	cups milk
¼	cup whipping cream
	zest or rind* from 1 medium orange (grated)
5	whole eggs
1	egg yolk
¾	cup sugar
	dash of salt (optional)
¼	cup Grand Marnier liqueur
6	T. Grand Marnier liqueur

— Caramel Syrup —

1. Combine sugar, water and cream of tartar in medium saucepan. Stir well.
2. Place over high heat. Stir constantly until mixture turns a dark brown color, approximately 10 minutes.
3. Carefully pour mixture into 6 one cup souffle dishes or custard cups. Swirl immediately to coat well and to partially cover sides.
4. Let stand at least 10 minutes to harden.

— Custard —

5. Combine milk, cream and orange zest in another medium saucepan.

— Continued —

200

6. Place over medium heat to warm.
7. Preheat oven to 325°. Put a kettle of water on to heat.
8. In small mixing bowl, beat eggs and egg yolk on low speed until blended.
9. Add sugar and salt and mix on low speed until smooth.
10. Add egg mixture to warming milk mixture, stirring well.
11. Add ¼ cup Grand Marnier and stir constantly over heat until custard mixture is hot.
12. Quickly pour custard through a strainer into each cup, filling all evenly.
13. Set cups in an oven proof pan and add boiling water to a 1" depth.
14. Set pan in preheated oven. Bake for 40 minutes.
15. Remove cups. Cool; cover; and refrigerate for 4 hours or more.
16. To unmold, run sharp knife around edge of each souffle cup.
17. Invert small plate over cup and quickly flip over.
18. Top each custard with 1 tablespoon Grand Marnier. Serve immediately.

Serves: 6
Preparation: 35 minutes
Cooking: 40 minutes
Cooling: 4 hours or longer

*See Zest in Glossary

Delicious version of the classic French dessert! Grand Marnier flavor is wonderful! Try it for a special occasion! Can be made a day ahead for a relaxed hostess!

WIENERSCHNITZEL

A LA - Rainbow Lodge

1	veal rib-eye cut into 6 (8 oz.) portions *
½	cup flour
	salt and pepper (to taste)
2	eggs beaten with equal amount of water
2 - 3	cups fresh bread crumbs
½	lb. butter (clarified **)
1	cup mushroom sauce (favorite recipe or packaged) ***
6	lemon wedges
½	cup parsley (chopped)

1. Pound the portions of rib-eye to one-eighth inch thickness. This will make a thin but huge veal scallop.
2. Combine flour, salt and pepper. Dredge veal in flour, shake off excess.
3. Place veal pieces in egg wash, one at a time, coat both sides.
4. Coat both sides in fresh bread crumbs and set aside.
5. Heat generous amount of clarified butter in large frying pan. When almost smoking, add veal.
6. Cook for two to three minutes or until golden. Turn over and complete cooking.
7. Serve over a small amount of mushroom sauce. Squeeze fresh lemon and sprinkle with chopped parsley.

Serves: 6
Preparation: 35 minutes

* These are Texas sized portions.
** See Glossary
*** This is simply brown gravy sauce with mushrooms.

This dish is wonderful!

REFLECTIONS

Located in The Worthington Hotel, (formerly the Americana), in downtown Fort Worth, Reflections is opposite Sundance Square and only a few blocks from the Convention Center and County Courthouse.

While brick streets and boat shops are within window's view, Reflections' decor seems less afield when viewed alongside The Worthington's atrium lobby, waterfalls and swimming pool.

Situated on the mezzanine level, one enters the glass doors and encounters an expansive, multi-level dining room that recalls 1930's New York Art Deco. Three dominant pillars, simulating tulips, bear dark green stems, salmon-colored petals and rise to a white lattice work ceiling with black backing. The room's highest levels are at the front and rear with the lowest level in the center. The ceiling areas located over each of the two highest levels are covered in gold leaf. Waist-high partitions compartmentalize many of the dining areas. Finally, two narrow, reflective waterways course the middle of the lowest level lengthwise.

The table settings were elegant with crisp, salmon-colored table cloths and napkins. An onyx-colored dinner plate was flanked by smaller white dishes. A shaded candle holder and slender black vase with pink tulip completed the setting.

I began my dinner with Tortilla Soup. Plenty of chicken, carrots, celery and tortilla chips were well simmered in hot chicken broth. Not highly seasoned and more of a homestyle variety, I found it very satisfying.

— Continued —

The Reflections Salad soon followed. Red cabbage, watercress, tomatoes and a very good house dressing with a mustard base were tastefully topped with freshly ground pepper.

A raspberry sorbet with mint leaves was then put before me; homemade with the freshest raspberries, it was full of fresh fruit flavor.

While prime beef and steaks headed the entrees, I settled on Breast of Duck in Ginger Sauce. An unusually colorful presentation of young carrots, asparagus spears and potato provided accompaniment.

Finally, enticed by the sorbet, I succumbed to the temptation of homemade ice cream and indulged in Bananas Foster.

It took some time for my conservative nature to accommodate itself to towering tulips and gold leaf. However, the conversant staff, mostly native to Fort Worth, eased the transition by relating their own initial reactions and further contributed to what proved a very pleasant evening.

With The Worthington's present combination of experience, youth, energy and interest, I have no doubt that regular patrons of Reflections will be increasingly pleased with the service and cuisine.

Reflections is located at 200 Main St. in Fort Worth.

OYSTERS ROCKEFELLER

A LA - Reflections

20	oysters, cleaned and shucked, save deep half of each shell.
1	small bag rock salt
¼	cup butter
1	large onion (finely diced)
1	clove garlic (minced)
2	bunches spinach (washed, well dried and chopped) or 10 oz. pkg. frozen chopped spinach (thawed and drained)
½	cup Pernod liqueur
2	cups Hollandaise sauce (favorite recipe or made from package)
1	lemon, cut in wedges

1. Preheat oven to 400°
2. Place oysters on half shell.
3. Spread rocksalt in bottom of broiler pan or oven proof dish. Top with oysters and refrigerate.
4. In small fry pan melt butter; saute onions and garlic until transparent, approximately 5 minutes.
5. Add spinach to onion mix and saute several minutes. Remove from pan.
6. Top each oyster with spinach mix.
7. Sprinkle Pernod over each oyster.
8. Heat oysters in oven for 15 minutes.
9. Remove from oven and top with Hollandaise sauce.
10. Brown under broiler for 1 - 2 minutes.
11. Serve hot on rock salt garnished with lemon wedges.

Serves: 4
Preparation time: 30 minutes

Oyster Rockefeller lovers will find Chef Vernaglia's version wonderful!

VEAL CHOPS POELEE AUX CHAMPIGNONS
Veal with Mushrooms

==

A LA - Reflections

¼	cup olive oil
1	cup flour
4	veal chops (8 - 10 oz. each)
1	cup sliced mushrooms
1	T. fresh morel mushrooms (optional)
1	shallot (finely chopped)
¼	cup white wine
½	cup whipping cream
¼	cup demi glace (a reduced brown gravy sauce) *
	salt and pepper (to taste)
2	T. butter
1	clove garlic (chopped)
1	lb. fresh spinach (washed, dried and torn)

1. Preheat oven to 350°.
2. Heat oil in large oven proof frying pan over medium high.
3. Dust chops with flour. Add to heated oil.
4. Brown well, approximately 5 - 8 minutes. Turn chops over.
5. Add mushrooms, morels and shallots.
6. Cover and place in oven. Cook for 20 minutes or until tender and done.
7. Remove pan from oven. Remove chops and keep warm.
8. Discard grease in fry pan. Add wine and cook over medium heat, scraping up any bits that stick to pan.
9. Add cream and demi glace. Cook to reduce by half. Season to taste with salt and pepper and keep warm.
10. In separate pan, melt butter over medium high heat. Add garlic and spinach. Saute just until spinach becomes wilted.

— Continued —

11.　　To serve, place spinach on 4 plates and top each with cooked chop. Pour sauce over all.

Serves: 4
Preparation: 45 minutes

*Simply cook ½ cup brown gravy 15 - 20 minutes until reduced in half and flavors are concentrated.

A wonderful combination! Makes a special meal!

FETTUCCINE WITH SMOKED SALMON AND CAPERS

A LA - Reflections

1	lb. fresh fettuccine noodles
2	T. butter (melted)
¾	cup whipping cream
¼	lb. smoked salmon (boneless and chopped)
1	T. capers
½	lb. freshly grated Parmesan cheese
1	t. nutmeg
	salt and pepper (to taste)

1. Cook fettuccine to al dente* state. Drain and return to pan over medium heat.
2. Pour melted butter over pasta and toss.
3. Add cream. Cook until cream is reduced by half.
4. Add chopped salmon and capers. Toss in Parmesan cheese.
5. Season with nutmeg, salt and pepper.
6. Serve hot.

Serves: 6
Preparation: 25 minutes

* See Glossary under "Al Dente"

Delightful flavor combination! Perfect for special occasions and so easy to prepare!

COLD AVOCADO SOUP

A LA - Reflections

4	medium avocados, very ripe (peeled and seeded)
1	shallot
1½	lemons (juice only)
2	cups chicken stock (refrigerated to make it thicker)
½	cup sour cream
⅔	cup mayonnaise
½	cup yogurt
1	cup buttermilk
	salt and white pepper (to taste)
½	t. thyme (or to taste)
	lemon peel (optional garnish) – or –
1	tomato (optional garnish – cut julienne ie: 1½" long thin strips)

1. Chill soup bowls in freezer. Chill large mixing bowl in freezer.
2. In blender or food processor, puree avocados and shallot.
3. While machine is running, gradually add lemon juice and chicken stock until well blended.
4. Pour into large chilled bowl. Stir in sour cream, mayonnaise, yogurt and buttermilk.
5. Season as desired with salt, pepper and thyme. If too thick, thin with additional stock or buttermilk.
6. Serve cold with garnish of lemon peel or julienne of tomato.

Yield: 1 quart
Serves: 8 as 1st course
Preparation time: 15 minutes

A marvelous 1st course for a hot summer night! A must for avocado lovers!

SHRIMP VERNAGLIA

A LA - Reflections

36	jumbo shrimp (cleaned and deveined)
1	cup flour
4	eggs (beaten)
¼	cup butter
¼	cup olive oil
1	cup white wine
1	cup fresh squeezed orange juice
¼	cup sherry
2	shallots (finely chopped)
3	cups whipping cream
	salt and white pepper (to taste)
¼	lb. fresh or frozen crabmeat (cooked)
2	T. chives (chopped)

1. Partially butterfly shrimp by cutting lengthwise thru body but leaving tail end intact. Dip in flour then in eggs.
2. In large skillet, melt butter over medium high flame. Add oil; heat until hot.
3. Cook shrimp in skillet until golden brown, approximately 3 minutes on each side. Remove shrimp and keep warm.
4. Discard oil in skillet. Return to heat.
5. Add wine, orange juice, sherry and shallots. Stir to loosen bits clinging to bottom of pan.
6. Reduce liquid by one half by cooking.
7. Add heavy cream; add salt and pepper if necessary.
8. Reduce liquid by one half again by cooking. Cream will become golden in color.
9. To serve, arrange six shrimp on each plate; cover with sauce. Top with crabmeat. Garnish with chives.

Serves: 6 as appetizer; 3 as dinner
Preparation time: 45 minutes

Delicious combination! Sure to win raves from friends.

BANANAS AL CORDIAL

A LA - Reflections

9	firm bananas
3	T. butter (melted)
1	cup packed brown sugar
¼	t. ground cloves
¼	t. ground ginger
1	t. ground cinnamon
4	oz. can crushed pineapple with juice
¼	cup rum

1. Preheat oven to 350°
2. Cut bananas in half. Split each half lengthwise.
3. Pour butter in large baking dish.
4. Dip each banana slice in brown sugar. Place on baking dish.
5. Combine remaining brown sugar with spices and spread over bananas.
6. Top bananas and brown sugar with crushed pineapple and half the juice.
7. Bake in oven for 15 minutes. Baste occasionally with remaining juice.
8. Remove from oven and pour rum over bananas.
9. Ignite* and serve dish flaming.

Serves: 6
Preparation: 30 minutes

* For information on step 9 see "Flambe" in glossary.

A wonderful light dessert after a heavy meal and unbeatable over vanilla ice cream!

J. SNITILY 86 ©

Rotisserie
for
Beef and Bird

The Rotisserie for Beef and Bird was established on Owner/Chef Joe Mannke's belief that the only way to develop a loyal clientele is to provide quality food and friendly, attentive service.

Built to the owner's specifications, the one-hundred-and-fifty seat, single story restaurant is situated around the large charcoal "pit" and rotisserie.

The menu features charcoal broiled or grilled meats, game birds and other fowl. The variety of the featured items plus the significance of the total menu necessitates amplification. The finest, prime, grain-fed beef cannot upstage wild and domesticated fowl including duck, turkey and capon; Goose with Apple Brown Betty and Pheasant with Grapes, Pine Nuts and Wild Mushroom Sauce. Entree accompaniments include fresh vegetables like eggplant au gratin, sauteed or poached squash, savoury wild rice and Idaho potatoes served with sour cream and bacon. Seafoods are available and include fresh mountain trout, jumbo Gulf shrimp, lump crabmeat and Louisiana Seafood Gumbo.

To provide finality to an already formidable menu the resident pastry chef deserves credit for the Rippled Chocolate Fudge Cake, Bread Pudding, the Cobbler of the Day and the Praline Ice Cream with Chocolate Hazelnut Sauce.

That Joe Mannke's efforts have been very successful seems indisputable. Over twenty-one-hundred customers surrender themselves to the "Rotisserie's" enticements in an average week and voluntarily advertise this dining discovery hither and yon.

Rotisserie for Beef and Bird is located at 2200 Wilcrest in Houston.

CREAM OF PHEASANT SOUP WITH PHEASANT DUMPLINGS

A LA - Rotisserie For Beef And Bird

1	pheasant (you can substitute 2 rock Cornish game hens)
2	bay leaves
	dash of salt
2	T. butter
½	small onion (coarsely chopped)
½	leek (coarsely chopped)
1	celery stalk (coarsely chopped)
2	T. flour
	dash of salt
	dash of white pepper
2	slices bread soaked in ½ cup cream
	dash of rosemary, marjoram, salt
1	t. parsley (chopped)
1	whole egg
1	cup whipping cream
¼	cup dry sherry

1. Remove uncooked meat from breast, thigh and leg bones; refrigerate.
2. Combine all bones and giblets with bay leaves, salt and 2 quarts water. Simmer for 2 hours or until liquid is reduced to four cups. Strain.
3. In large skillet, melt butter. Saute onion, leek and celery for 5 minutes over low heat.
4. Add flour, salt and pepper. Mix well.
5. Gradually add the 4 cups hot broth, stirring constantly. Simmer for 35 minutes.
6. Next make the dumplings. In processor or meat grinder, grind reserved pheasant meat very fine.

— Continued —

7. Grind cream soaked bread.
8. Combine meat, bread, seasonings and egg. Grind again.
9. Keeping hands wet, shape mixture into small meatballs 1" in diameter.
10. Simmer for 5 minutes in boiling salted water. Remove and keep warm.
11. Strain pheasant soup. Return to pot. Add cream, sherry and dumplings. Reheat; do not boil.
12. Serve hot.

Serves: 6
Preparation: 45 minutes
Cooking: 2 hours

A rich first course!

VENISON* STEW
(Begin at least 24 hours ahead)

A LA - Rotisserie For Beef And Bird

— Basic Marinade for Venison — *

1	cup dry sherry
½	cup vinegar
½	cup water
½	carrot (chopped)
½	stalk celery (chopped)
½	medium onion (chopped)
2	cloves garlic
½	t. peppercorn (crushed)
2	t. pickling spices

— Stew —

2½	lbs. marinated venison * (cubed)
¼	cup butter
1	t. salt
	dash of pepper
1	small onion (coarsely chopped)
1	stalk celery (coarsely chopped)
2	T. tomato paste
½	cup dry red wine
1	cup canned or packaged beef gravy
1	cup reserved marinade
2	slices bacon (diced)
½	lb. mushrooms (sliced)
12	pearl onions (boiled or canned)
1	cup croutons (toasted)
1	T. red currant jelly
1.	T. whipping cream

— Continued —

1. Combine all marinade ingredients and pour over venison. Marinate overnight or longer.
2. Preheat oven to 325°.
3. Drain venison. Strain and reserve marinade.
4. Melt butter in frying pan. Saute venison until browned on both sides and transfer to casserole.
5. Add salt, pepper, vegetables, tomato paste, red wine, beef gravy and 1 cup reserved marinade.
6. Simmer slowly in oven for 2 hours.
7. Meanwhile, saute bacon; add mushrooms, onions and toasted croutons. Set aside and keep warm.
8. Remove venison from gravy. Keep warm.
9. Strain gravy through sieve and return to casserole.
10. Stir in jelly and cream. Reheat. Do not boil.
11. To serve, pour sauce over venison and cover with mushroom crouton mixture.

Serves: 6
Preparation: 35 minutes
Baking: 2 hours

* If venison is unavailable, lamb or grain fed calf can be used.

This is a delicious marinade and stew! Great for any stew meat. Chef suggests serving with wild rice or noodles.

ROAST GOOSE WITH STEWED APPLES

A LA - Rotisserie For Beef And Bird

1	goose, 6 - 8 lbs.
	salt and pepper (to taste)
2	T. marinated green peppercorns (in grocery gourmet or relish section)
2	apples (peeled, cored and diced)
2	stalks celery (chopped)
1	carrot (chopped)
2	small onions (chopped)
1	20 oz. can stewed apples
2	T. light brown sugar
1	cup raisins
½	t. cinnamon
½	cup dry white wine
1	t. lemon juice
2	t. arrowroot or cornstarch

1. Preheat oven to 350°.
2. Remove giblets from goose. Rub cavity with salt and pepper.
3. Crush peppercorns; mix with apples. Stuff goose with mixture; place goose in roasting pan. Surround goose with mixture of celery, carrot and onions. Add one cup water.
4. Place in oven and roast for one and one half hours. Baste occasionally.
5. When goose is done, remove meat from breast and leg bones. Keep warm.
6. Chop bones; return to roasting pan. Add one cup water. Simmer this gravy for 30 minutes, stirring and scraping up residue in bottom of pan.

— Continued —

218

7.   Meanwhile, put canned apples in separate saucepan. Add brown sugar, raisins, cinnamon, wine and lemon juice. Simmer gently for five minutes. Keep warm.

8.   Remove gravy from heat. Strain and thicken with arrow-root if necessary.

9.   To serve, place hot apple sauce on large platter. Slice goose meat and arrange over sauce. Serve gravy on side.

Serves: 6
Preparation: 45 minutes
Baking: 1 hour 30 minutes

This dish is wonderful for a festive meal. The flavors are so complementary.

TEXAS STEAK SALAD
(Begin 3 hours ahead)

A LA - Rotisserie For Beef And Bird

2½	lbs. lean, tender, trimmed beef (cooked) (roast beef, etc.)
2	small onions (sliced and separated into rings)
½	cup wine vinegar
¾	cup olive oil
1	T. capers
2	T. fresh parsley (chopped)
1	t. chopped tarragon or ½ t. dry tarragon
2	t. chives (chopped)
1	T. pimento (chopped)
2	hard cooked eggs (chopped)
¼	t. dry mustard
	dash of freshly ground black pepper
1	head iceberg lettuce (cut into ½ inch squares)
1	head romaine (cut in ½ inch squares)
1	avocado (peeled and sliced)
2	ripe tomatoes (cut in wedges)

1. Thinly slice beef across grain and place in large bowl.
2. Spread onions over beef.
3. Combine vinegar, oil, capers, herbs, pimento, eggs, mustard and pepper. Stir to blend. Pour over beef.
4. Refrigerate for at least three hours.
5. Combine meat mixture with lettuce in salad bowl. Garnish with avocado and tomato and serve.

Serves: 6 - 8 generously
Marinate: 3 hours
Preparation: 10 minutes

Delicious!

220

ROAST RACK OF LAMB WITH HERBS AND GARLIC BREAD CRUMBS

A LA - Rotisserie For Beef And Bird

2	racks of lamb (each 1 - 1½ lbs. with any excessive fat removed)
1	T. salt
2	T. "fines herbs" (purchase in grocery spice section)
1	t. tarragon
1	t. chives
1	t. shallots
1	t. parsley
½	cup bread crumbs
1	T. chopped parsley
2	cloves garlic (peeled and minced)

1. Preheat oven to 450°.
2. Rub meat all over with salt. Score or make narrow cuts into remaining fat. Rub in fines herbs and next four herbs, on all surfaces of meat.
3. Roast lamb racks in oven, fat side down, for 25 minutes.
4. Combine bread crumbs, parsley and garlic. When lamb finishes baking, sprinkle over top side of rack and roast for 5 minutes longer.
5. Remove, cut up and serve immediately.

Serves: 4
Preparation: 15 minutes
Baking: 30 minutes

The flavor of this dish is perfect!

STRAWBERRIES ROMANOFF

(Begin 90 minutes ahead)

═══════════════════════════════

A LA - Rotisserie For Beef And Bird

1	pt. fresh, firm, ripe strawberries – plus (see last ingredient)
2	T. Grand Marnier
1	T. Kirsch
4	T. brown sugar (packed)
1	orange (juiced) or ½ cup orange juice
1	cup whipping cream
2	T. confectioners sugar
1	cup vanilla ice cream (slightly softened)
6	large strawberries for garnish and six green leaves (optional garnish)

1. Place 2 bowls in freezer to chill.
    Wash and dry strawberries. Hull and thinly slice. Place berries in a well chilled bowl.
2. Add Grand Marnier, Kirsch and brown sugar. Toss until berries are well coated.
3. Add orange juice; cover tightly with saran wrap and chill 1 hour, in refrigerator.
4. Meanwhile, into another well chilled bowl, pour cream and whip until stiff peaks form. Add confectioners sugar and ice cream. Mix well.
5. Combine cream mixture and strawberries.
6. Serve in individual dessert glasses. Garnish each dish with whole berry and green leaf.

Serves: 4 - 6
Preparation: 30 minutes
Refrigeration: 1 hour

Absolutely divine dessert. A must in strawberry season.

Sergio & Luciano Ristorante Italiano

Sergio & Luciano in Dallas' Addison section, is thought by more than just a few knowledgeable types to be one of the most radiant stones in Dallas' corona of fine Italian restaurants.

The efforts of Sergio Burone and Luciano Cola reflect talents which extend beyond the kitchen. The restaurant's two floors reveal an ability to utilize lighting to produce chamelionesque color changes from lunch to dinner. Swag curtains, ceiling fans and tasteful selections in wallpaper and carpeting create an atmosphere that assures receptivity and relaxation.

Atmosphere notwithstanding, the cuisine is the obvious allure. Appetizers present homemade pasta including creamed fettucini with ham and sliced mushrooms and tortellini with a chicken liver pate.

Italian cuisine does not have to begin with Sergio's pasta and end with the obligatory cappuccino. At lunch, the salads are unusually alluring. Insalata Primavera presents a diadem of julienne of chicken over cold pasta in a garlic and ginger dressing. Total freshness is in keeping with a fine restaurant and upon consuming this panoply of color, a feeling of resusitation isn't all in the mind.

Fresh fish, deftly sauteed with lemon; tender veal in a marsala sauce and delicate chicken are all likely to be served in consort with fresh, well-tended, al dente vegetables. Pasta entrees are no less captivating than the appetizers and include a popular Lasagna Verde and a manicotti filled with fresh ricotta.

— Continued —

Desserts offer spumoni, Cappuccino Pie and the very popular, if oddly dubbed Zuppa Inglese. The latter is composed of custard, a spongecake-like bread and caramel. It is usually still warm from baking and bears a whipped cream and strawberry garniture.

Finally, the staff reflects the Italian tradition for cordialita and servizievole.

Sergio & Luciano is located at 4900 Beltline Road in Dallas.

INSALATA TENTAZIONE
Delectable Salad

A LA - Sergio & Luciano

¼	head red cabbage (shredded)
	Boston lettuce leaves
1	avocado (peeled and sliced evenly)
1	papaya (seeded, peeled and sliced evenly)
1	mango (peeled and sliced evenly)
3	T. olive oil
1½	T. fresh lime juice
½	t. sugar
	pinch of oregano
	salt and white pepper (to taste)
2	T. chopped walnuts

1. Arrange red cabbage and Boston lettuce leaves on a platter.
2. Arrange avocado slices in the center and the papaya and mango slices on either side of the avocado.
3. Mix thoroughly: oil, lime juice, sugar, oregano, salt and pepper.
4. Pour dressing over the avocado, mango and papaya. Sprinkle with chopped walnuts.

Serves: 2 generously
Preparation: 10 minutes

A wonderful combination!

ARTICHOKES EDUARDO
(Begin several hours in advance)

A LA - Sergio & Luciano

4	**fresh artichokes**
2	**T. flour**
¼	**cup lemon juice**
2	**T. olive oil**

½	**cup olive oil**
¼	**cup red wine vinegar**
2	**T. yellow onion (chopped)**
1	**T. red pimiento (chopped)**
1	**t. parsley (chopped)**
1	**t. capers (chopped)**
	white of hard boiled egg (finely chopped)
	salt and pepper (to taste)
	red cabbage leaves (garnish)

1. Clean and wash artichokes. Remove stems.
2. Mix flour, lemon juice, oil and enough water to cover artichokes in a large pan and bring to a boil.
3. Add artichokes and cook until tender, approximately 40 minutes. Base of leaves will be tender and soft to eat. Cool in water.
4. Cut artichokes in half and remove chokes * . Put artichokes on one large plate.
5. Mix oil, vinegar and remaining ingredients except garnish; whisk together until mixture becomes thick. Pour over artichokes and refrigerate until cold.
6. Arrange cabbage leaves on individual serving plates. Place artichokes on top and serve, making sure you scrape all the sauce onto artichokes.

— Continued —

226

Serves: 4 whole or 8 halves
Preparation: 15 minutes
Cooking Time: 30 - 40 minutes

* These are the center leaves and hairy fibers which are hard to eat. To remove, work your fingers into center and pull out leaves. Remove hairy fibers by scraping them out with tip of sharp edged spoon or knife.

A wonderful salad or 1st course!

J. SNITILY 86 ©

tony's

Much has been said of Tony's and virtually all has been in the superlative. One noted restaurant critic designated the main dining room as "one of the most beautiful in America." The wine cellar has been described as "one of the most notable in America," and information has it that "some of the most magnificent dinner parties in the South's history" have taken place within arm's length of more than 100,000 imported wines.

Located on Houston's Post Oak Boulevard, Tony's three dining rooms offer tiers of fresh flowers, original paintings, antique Chinese porcelain and a three-hundred year old Chinese silk screen.

A staff of over sixty-five, most visible being waiters in starched whites and black ties, orchestrates its energies to bring to the table only the highest quality and freshest foods available.

Although the cuisine is mainly Classic French, the a la carte menu also offers Mediterranean, Northern Italian, and contemporary dishes.

Over a dozen appetizers include several caviar selections, smoked Nova Scotia salmon, a scallop mousse, and two varieties of scampi.

The velvety Lobster Bisque and the Vichyssoise are soups that

— Continued —

stir your enthusiasm.

Entrees provide excellent diversity. The Broiled Rack of Lamb and the Whole Roast Duckling head the list and each is a dinner for two. Filet of Sole and three varieties of Red Snapper, including the Red Snapper Noisette, insure clear recollections. The Poulet Brasserie is a savory representative of the poultry family.

Tony's, with its numerous awards and recognitions warrants reservations for either lunch or dinner.

Tony's is located at 1801 Post Oak Blvd. in Houston.

OYSTERS BEACH HOUSE

A LA - Tony's

½   cup butter
¼   cup green onions (chopped)
¼   cup mushrooms (sliced)
1   t. dry mustard
    pinch of cayenne
¾   cup flour
2   cups milk
½   cup dry sherry
2   egg yolks (beaten)
2   dozen raw oysters (shucked and cleaned) Reserve half
    of the shells.

1. Preheat oven to 350°.
2. Melt butter in saucepan.
3. Saute green onions, mushrooms, mustard and cayenne
    in butter.
4. Add flour and cook for 3 - 4 minutes, stirring continually.
5. Gradually add milk. Cook and stir for 8 - 10 minutes.
6. Add sherry. Remove from heat.
7. Stir a small amount of sauce into egg yolks. Pour egg
    mixture back into sauce and stir well.
8. Place each raw oyster in reserved shells. Put shells in
    baking pan.
9. Cover each oyster with sauce.
10. Bake for 10 - 12 minutes until sauce is lightly brown on
    top.

Serves: 4
Preparation: 40 minutes

**Delicious first course! Even non-oyster lovers raved about this
dish!**

SHRIMP TONY'S

A LA - Tony's

24	large shrimp (butterflied with tail left on)*
6	T. butter
3	or 4 garlic cloves (minced)
2	cups fresh mushrooms (sliced and patted dry)
1½	cups whipping cream
1	T. tomato paste
6	T. sweet sherry
1	T. tarragon
	salt and pepper (to taste)
	cayenne pepper
1	T. dried basil or handful of fresh basil
3	T. brandy

1. Clean, shell and butterfly shrimp.
2. Melt butter in saucepan over medium heat. Add garlic and saute 3 - 4 minutes.
3. Add shrimp and saute just until they turn color, about 2 - 3 minutes each side. Remove shrimp and add mushrooms. Saute mushrooms and remove.
4. Next add cream and tomato paste, sherry, tarragon and salt and pepper to taste. Let simmer until sauce is slightly thickened, about 20 - 30 minutes.
5. Return shrimp and mushrooms to pan and add a pinch or two of cayenne. Add basil (tear fresh basil into pieces, it is recommended over the dry).
6. Add brandy; tip pan and ignite or flambe and serve.*

---

* See Glossary for more instructions if needed on how to "butterfly" shrimp and how to "flambe".

Serves: 4
Cooking: 30 minutes
Preparation: 15 minutes

Chef suggests serving shrimp and sauce over toast points in the center of a seasoned rice ring. Absolutely yummy!

CORNISH GAME HENS DIABLO

A LA - Tony's

4	Cornish Game Hens (thawed)
1	pkg. seasoned Wild Rice (cooked) *
½	lb. fresh mushrooms (finely chopped)
1	cup chicken bouillon

— Diablo Sauce —

¼	cup olive oil
1	scallion (chopped)
1	garlic clove (minced)
1	t. fresh Chervil or parsley (finely chopped)
1	t. cracked black pepper
½	cup brandy or sherry
2	t. worchestershire sauce
1	t. dry English mustard
2 - 3	drops Tabasco
2	cups brown gravy (you can buy prepared mix in packets)
	juice of one lemon
2	T. catsup
	paprika (for garnish)
	butter (for garnish)

1. Preheat oven to 400°.
2. Cook rice according to package directions. Meanwhile, clean hens with water and pat dry. Clean, dry and chop mushrooms.
3. Stuff game hens with seasoned, cooked rice and mushrooms. Close the opening with skewers.
4. Place hens in a greased baking dish with bouillon. Cover and bake in preheated 400° oven for 25 minutes or until tender.

— Continued —

234

━━━━━━━━━━━━━━━━━━━━━━━━━━━━━
━━━━━━━━━━━━━━━━━━━━━━━━━━━━━

—Diablo Sauce—

5. While hens are baking, heat oil in a fry pan and saute scallion, garlic and parsley. When they are soft, add the remaining ingredients, except paprika and butter, and simmer slowly for about 10 minutes. Keep hot.
6. When hens are baked, remove them from oven and sprinkle with a touch of paprika and coat with butter. Place them under preheated broiler and brown until golden. Remove hens to platter; pour Diablo Sauce over and serve.

Serves: 4
Preparation: 50 minutes (including cooking rice)

* A 6 oz. package of Uncle Ben's Seasoned Wild Rice will adequately stuff four hens. You may, however, want to prepare additional rice to serve on the side as it's a wonderful accompaniment.

STUFFED PORK CHOPS WITH APPLES & PECANS

A LA - Tony's

6	¾" thick pork chops (trimmed of fat)
	salt and pepper
¼	cup oil
½	cup flour
3	cooking apples (cored, peeled, finely chopped)
1½	cups soft bread crumbs
¾	cup celery (chopped)
¼	cup milk
3	T. soft butter
	pinch of sage
	pinch of allspice
½	cup chopped pecans
	toothpicks or scewers

1. Preheat oven to 350°
2. Lay pork chops flat and make parallel cut thru center of chop, right up to bone for stuffing.
3. Season all sides of chops with salt and pepper. Heat oil in large frying pan.
4. Dip each chop in flour and brown lightly in hot oil for approximately 10 minutes.
5. Combine remaining ingredients to make stuffing. Season with more salt and pepper to taste.
6. Equally divide stuffing between pork chops. Stuff well. Close with skewers.
7. Place stuffed chops in large buttered baking dish. Bake for 30 minutes; remove skewers and serve.

Serves: 6
Preparation: 30 minutes
Baking: 30 minutes

A hearty winter dish! Good flavor combination!

CRANBERRY SORBET WITH KIWI*

A LA - Tony's

2	12 oz. packages fresh cranberries (washed)
2	cups water
1½	cups sugar
¼	cup fresh orange juice
2	T. lime juice
2	T. cranberry liqueur or kirsch
6	kiwi fruit (peeled and thinly sliced)

1. Combine cranberries and water in saucepan. Cover.
2. Cook over medium high heat until berries pop, approximately three minutes. Drain well.
3. Transfer berries to blender or processor.
4. Add sugar, orange juice, lime juice and liqueur. Puree until smooth.
5. Press mixture through sieve into medium bowl. Let cool.
6. Transfer to ice cream maker and freeze according to manufacturers directions - or - put into freezer and stir every 30 minutes to break up large ice crystals. After 3-4 hours, whisk until smooth.
7. To serve, arrange kiwi fruit in a circular pattern on individual plates. Scoop sorbet into centers. Serve immediately.

Serves: 6
Preparation: 45 minutes, plus freezing time

* Sorbets are also called Water Ices - similar to sherbet.

A delightfully refreshing dessert! Very colorful to serve!

ILE FLOTTANTE AUX PRALINES
Floating Island with Pralines

A LA - Tony's

½	cup sugar
2	T. water
	pinch of cream of tartar
4	large egg whites, at room temperature
	pinch of cream of tartar
⅔	cup sugar
½	t. vanilla
⅓	cup Crushed Praline Candies *
4	T. Crushed Pralines (for garnish) *
2	cups Vanilla Custard Sauce (cooked) *

1. Preheat oven to 275°.
2. In a heavy saucepan combine sugar, water and one pinch of cream of tartar over low heat.
3. Stir and wash down sugar crystals with a brush dipped in cold water until sugar dissolves.
4. Cook mixture over medium heat, without stirring until mixture is a deep caramel color.
5. Pour into a four cup greased mold. Let cool for 30 seconds or until slightly thickened. Tilt mold to coat bottom and sides completely.
6. In separate bowl, beat egg whites with cream of tartar until soft peaks form. Slowly beat in sugar, a little at a time. Add vanilla.
7. Continue beating until meringue forms stiff peaks.
8. Spoon half of meringue into mold. Sprinkle with Crushed Pralines (recipe follows).
9. Cover with remaining meringue. Smooth top with spatula.
10. Put mold in baking pan. Pour hot water in pan to reach halfway up sides of mold.

— Continued —

11. Bake in middle of oven for 40 minutes or until toothpick inserted comes out clean.
12. Remove from oven and invert on serving platter. Sprinkle with Crushed Pralines. Serve with Vanilla Custard (recipe on following pages) over and around individual servings.

Serves: 4
Preparation: 1 hour

(The two following recipes for Crushed Pralines and Vanilla Custard Sauce take a total of 1 hour preparation plus 3 hours refrigeration)

*See "Crushed Praline" and "Vanilla Custard Sauce" recipes on the next two pages. They are both part of this recipe but can be used on their own to enhance other dishes.

A novel method of preparing a traditional French favorite. A very impressive dessert!

CRUSHED PRALINES

(part of Tony's Floating Island Dessert on the preceding page
– or can be used on its own as a topping)

A LA - Tony's

1   **cup sugar**
¼   **cup water**
        pinch cream of tartar
1   **cup sliced blanched almonds**

1.   In a heavy skillet combine sugar, water and cream of tartar.
2.   Bring mixture to boil over moderately high heat.
3.   Stir often and wash down sugar crystals with a brush dipped in cold water.
4.   When sugar dissolves, cook mixture over medium heat, without stirring, until it turns a light caramel color. This will take about ten minutes.
5.   Add almonds and swirl pan until nuts are well coated.
6.   Pour out onto a buttered piece of foil and allow to cool and harden.
7.   On a board, chop the praline coarsely.
8.   In a blender or food processor crush praline pieces in batches.
9.   Store in airtight container.

Makes: 2 cups
Preparation: 30 minutes

Great over Tony's Floating Island or as topping for ice creams!

VANILLA CUSTARD SAUCE

(part of Tony's Floating Island Dessert, on page 238 – or can be used alone)
(Chill for at least three hours)

A LA - Tony's

4	large egg yolks
⅓	cup sugar
2	cups half and half (scalded)
1½	t. vanilla
1½	t. Grand Marnier (optional)

1. Beat egg yolks and sugar with electric mixer until mixture thickens and ribbons form when beater is lifted.
2. In a slow steady stream add scalded half and half, beating continuously.
3. Pour mixture into a heavy saucepan. Cook custard over moderately low heat stirring constantly until it thickens. DO NOT BOIL or it will curdle.
4. Pour sauce into a bowl, stir in vanilla and Grand Marnier. Cover with buttered waxpaper.
5. Let cool. Chill for at least three hours.

Makes: 2 cups
Preparation: 30 minutes
Refrigeration: 3 hours or more

A delicious light custard! Serve over Tony's Floating Island Dessert (page 238), fresh or canned fruit, or warm pies and cobblers.

J. SNITILY 86 ©

VARGO'S

Located on Fondren Road, north of Westheimer, Vargo's is presently on Houston's commercial periphery and provided me a welcome interlude from the unbridled din of urbanization.

Its fourteen acres included a lake, substantial pines, various types of deciduous trees, euonymus, magnolia and well-nourished lawns on all sides. Grey squirrels and peacocks foraged among the leaves, while various types of water fowl enlivened the lake and its shoreline.

As light was fading and the peacocks sought their night's refuge in the large trees, I entered Vargo's hoping for a table from which to continue observing the outdoor proceedings.

Floor-to-ceiling windows were liberally dispersed through most of Vargo's dining and lounge areas. The main dining room made the greatest accommodation to those who derive equal sustenance from flora and fauna. Glass windows rose to vaulted ceiling. Anchored at the center of the room was a tree of substantial girth that continued beyond the ceiling's limits. Vines and moss clothed its trunk and lush fronds encircled its base.

The ducks having dozed off within view of my table, I turned my attention to a relish tray that included a mixture of cooked zucchini, tomato and mushrooms, other sliced vegetables,

— Continued —

cheddar cheeses, pasta and herring. Moments later, a basket of homemade bread and a side dish of Bing Cherry Sauce appeared.

Four large shrimp, bathed in butter and parsley, were served hot and ably represented a selection of appetizers that included French Onion Soup Au Gratin, Escargot, Shrimp Cocktail, Soup du Jour and a crabmeat plate.

A basket of warm, very delicious rolls were served under linen along with a generous green salad that included tomato, carrots, grated bleu cheese and a vinegar and oil dressing.

Entrees included fish, duck, chicken, lamb and several varieties of beef including Prime Rib, New York Sirloin and Filet Mignon. I chose Veal Zingara and reveled in my selection. The portion seemed substantial. Tender veal, served in a light sauce, was liberally accompanied by sauteed mushrooms, green olives, julienne ham, pimento and a side order of lightly buttered linguini. I seldom order veal, but I would recommend this very creative mingling to most anyone. Veal, mushrooms and linguini work well together, but without seasoning can often lack distinction. The lightly salted ham and the green olives with pimento added a tang that, while not overbearing, further characterized the whole.

If the above items seemed sufficient, let me say that there also were side dishes of spiced apples, delicious mashed potatoes served with an equally fine gravy, green beans, dirty rice and more warm rolls.

Finishing in style, I requested the Chocolate Roll, a chocolate cake intertwined with cream and covered with a chocolate sauce and sliced almonds.

In summary, I would suggest visiting Vargo's when hunger or the city's turmoil have taken their toll. Serving lunch and dinner, with entertainment nightly, Vargo's is a source of serenity and quality cuisine that I wish Houston's commercial envelopment would leave undisturbed.

Vargo's is located at 2401 Fondren in Houston.

VEAL ZINGARA

A LA - Vargo's

2	4 oz. portions veal loin (flattened) seasoned with salt and pepper
2	oz. butter
¼	cup flour
4	large white mushrooms (thinly sliced)
4	large stuffed green olives (thinly sliced)
2	oz. smoked beef tongue or smoked beef (cut into very thin strips)
½	cup dry sherry
4	oz. butter (cut in pieces)
1	T. green onions (chopped)
1	T. parsley (chopped)

1. Preheat oven to warm.
2. Melt 2 oz. of butter in a fry pan.
3. Dip seasoned veal in flour and coat both sides.
4. Saute veal until lightly brown on both sides.
5. Remove veal from pan to a platter and keep warm in oven.
6. Add mushrooms, olives and tongue to pan. Saute for a few minutes.
7. Add sherry and let it reduce by cooking a few more minutes.
8. Remove pan from heat and slowly add pieces of butter all the while stirring, until they are melted and incorporated into sauce. Add the onions and parsley. Stir. Next add veal. Serve immediately.

Serves: 2
Preparation: 25 minutes

A wonderful combination! Serve the sauce over buttered noodles, spaghetti or rice pilaf!

245

CHOCOLATE ROLL - SPECIALTY OF THE HOUSE

A LA - Vargo's

12	egg yolks (save whites)
2¾	cup powered sugar
4	T. powdered cocoa
1	t. vanilla
12	egg whites
1	T. powdered sugar
1½	pints whipping cream
¼	cup sugar
1	T. vanilla
1	cup chocolate syrup
½	cup toasted almonds (chopped)

1. Preheat oven to 475°.
2. Prepare jelly roll pan * by greasing well, lining with parchment paper and greasing paper well.
3. Using electric mixer, beat egg yolks, powdered sugar, cocoa and vanilla until smooth. Set aside.
4. In another bowl, beat egg whites until very stiff.
5. Fold egg yolk mixture into egg whites and pour into prepared pan.
6. Bake 10 minutes.
7. Dust tea towel lightly with powered sugar.
8. Remove cake from oven and invert onto tea towel. Let cool.
9. Whip cream, sugar and vanilla together. Do not over whip.
10. Spread completely over cake. Roll cake lengthwise into roll using towel to help roll, and refrigerate at least 1 hour, or until ready to serve.
11. To serve, slice cake and top with chocolate syrup and toasted chopped almonds.

— Continued —

Serves: 6
Preparation: 25 minutes
Baking: 10 minutes

*Any large rectangular shallow pan will do. We used a
10 x 15 x 1 inch cookie sheet.

Serve this for a festive occasion! Actually light tasting!

SCAMPI GIOVANNI

A LA - Vargo's

½	lb. butter
4	cloves garlic (ground or crushed)
	juice of one lemon
16	shrimp (peel, clean and butterfly*)

1. Preheat oven to broil.
2. Combine butter and garlic in sauce pan. Add lemon juice to your taste. Saute over medium heat.
3. Arrange shrimp in shallow broiler pan. Pour sauce over shrimp.
4. Broil for five minutes. Serve immediately.

Serves: 4
Preparation: 10 minutes

* See Glossary of Terms if you need more directions on how to "butterfly" shrimp.

Simple, elegant and delicious!

WE REMEMBER . . .

The CARLYLE, Nick's Fishmarket and *Jean-Claude* are now closed, but they were three wonderful restaurants we remember in Houston and the latter in Dallas, for their arrestingly beautiful interiors and unexcelled food.

The Carlyle was one of the few restaruants to appear in Architectural Digest, (Sept. 1983) an eight page spread featuring its preponderance of mirrors, marbles and silks.

Chef Jean Claude, of the restaurant that bore his name, has displayed his skills on national television and has been written about in such prestigious journals as the New York times. He's one of those great chefs we will continue hearing about in the future.

In the pages that follow, you will enjoy some of the recipes that made these restaurants famous. You'll then know why we felt it incumbent upon us to include them. So although you can't dine there at present, their legacy will continue at your table with the following recipes.

FETTUCCINE ALFREDO

A LA - The Carlyle

2	**cups whipping cream**
1	**T. unsalted butter**
4	**oz. Parmesan cheese (grated)**
½	**lb. fettuccine**

1. Over low heat, slowly cook and reduce cream by one half, until creamy.
2. Add butter and cheese; stir until dissolved. Keep warm.
3. Boil pasta to al dente*. Drain and cool in cold water for three minutes.
4. Mix pasta into sauce. Season with salt and pepper. Serve immediately.

Serves: 4
Preparation: 25 minutes

* See Glossary

A very rich pasta dish! Also an excellent base for Seafood or Vegetable Fettuccine. Add your favorite ingredients if you wish! And remember, the trick to excellent pasta is FRESH GRATED PARMESAN!

CRAB PIGNON

A LA - The Carlyle

1	lb. lump crabmeat
¼	cup pine nuts
1	T. unsalted butter
1	T. shallots (minced)
1	T. green onions (minced)
½	cup chablis wine
¼	cup unsalted butter
1	T. lemon juice

1. Saute crabmeat and pine nuts in butter until warm.
2. Add shallots and green onions and cook over low heat for five minutes.
3. Heat wine, butter and lemon juice. Whisk until well combined.
4. Pour wine over crabmeat and serve.

Serves: 4
Preparation: 10 minutes

A wonderfully simple dish to serve on special occasions.

RED SNAPPER GABRIEL

A LA - The Carlyle

4	(8 oz.) snapper fillets
⅓	cup flour
¼	cup unsalted butter
½	lb. headless shrimp (cleaned and deveined)
¼	lb. crabmeat
5	small artichoke hearts (sliced)
1	lb. fresh mushrooms (sliced)
¼	cup almonds (sliced)
2	T. green onions (minced)
¼	cup unsalted butter
½	cup sauterne wine
⅛	cup capers

1. Dust snapper with flour and saute on both sides in melted butter until golden. Keep warm.
2. In a separate pan, combine shrimp, crabmeat, artichokes, mushrooms, almonds and onions. Cook slowly in melted butter for ten minutes.
3. Add wine and capers and pour over snapper and serve.

Serves: 4
Preparation: 15 minutes

A yummy combination!

VEAL FRANCAISE

A LA - The Carlyle

1¼	lb. veal loin (sliced into two ounce portions)
	salt and pepper (to taste)
¼	cup unsalted butter
12	artichoke hearts (sliced)
2	lbs. mushrooms (sliced)
1	cup demi-glace * or rich brown gravy
1	cup white wine
1	lb. unsalted butter
1	T. lemon juice

1. Pound veal into thin medallions. Season with salt and pepper.
2. Melt butter in large frying pan and saute veal quickly on both sides.
3. Add artichoke hearts and mushrooms. Saute.
4. Add demi-glace, white wine and butter. Stir until sauce is creamy.
5. Add lemon juice. Season to taste with salt and pepper and serve.

Serves: 6
Preparation: 15 minutes

* See Glossary

A very simple, elegant entree.

CREAM A LA RUSSE STRAWBERRIES
(Grand Marnier Cream over Berries)

A LA - The Carlyle

1	pint whipping cream
2	pkgs. unflavored gelatin
¼	cup cold water
2	cups sugar
½	lb. sour cream
½ - 1	cup Grand Marnier Liqueur
1	quart strawberries (hulled and washed)

1. Cook cream over medium heat until reduced by half, stirring constantly.
2. Dissolve gelatin in cold water.
3. Add sugar and gelatin to reduced cream. Cook over low heat for 10 minutes or until sugar and gelatin have been dissolved and are well mixed.
4. Stir in sour cream and Grand Marnier. Cool in refrigerator.
5. Serve over strawberries.

Serves: 4
Preparation: 45 minutes
Refrigeration: 1 hour or more

A divine dessert - rich and creamy and laden with Grand Marnier. Test kitchen thought it was wonderful and easy.

GARLIC BUTTER

A LA - Nick's Fishmarket

½	lb. butter (softened)
½	cup fresh parsley (finely chopped)
1	T. brandy
2	T. white wine
2	dashes Tabasco sauce
2	dashes Angostura bitters (available in your grocery store's condiment section)
2	dashes Worcestershire sauce
2	cloves garlic (finely chopped)

1. Combine all ingredients and cook over low heat until butter is melted.
2. Continue to simmer, being careful not to brown butter or garlic until garlic is soft and well cooked.
3. Serve warm over ingredients of your choice.

Yield: 1 cup
Preparation: 15 minutes

Great flavor! Delicious over cooked shrimp and crab or spaghetti and other pastas.

MAHI MAHI HOUSTON STYLE

A LA - Nick's Fishmarket

1	t. olive oil
1	large onion (diced)
½	lb. mushrooms (diced)
2	tomatoes (peeled and diced)
½	large zucchini (cut julienne or thin french fry - like strips)
½	t. thyme
	pinch of white pepper
2	T. white wine
½	cup demi-glace (see recipe next page)
½	T. cornstarch - optional
½	cup vegetable oil
8	4 oz. filets of mahi-mahi (dolphin) *

1. Heat olive oil; add onions; saute until brown.
2. Add mushrooms and tomatoes and saute for 5 minutes.
3. Add zucchini, thyme, pepper and white wine.
4. Combine with demi-glace. (recipe next page)
5. Combine cornstarch with small amount of water and add to sauce to thicken slightly. Keep sauce warm.
6. Heat vegetable oil and saute filets 4 minutes on each side.
7. Place two filets on each plate and top with sauce.

Serves: 4
Preparation: 20 minutes

* Mahi-Mahi is delicious, moist and firm. If you desire, however, you may substitute cod.

A crisp combination of vegetables over a tasty fish!

256

DEMI-GLACE

A LA - Nick's Fishmarket

2	cubes beef boullion
2½	cups boiling water
2	sprigs parsley
¼	cup butter
6	T. flour
1	t. soy sauce

1. Dissolve boullion in boiling water. Add parsley and simmer 10 minutes.
2. Remove parsley and return to a boil.
3. In another pan, melt butter and stir in flour to make a thick paste.
4. Add mixture to boiling boullion. Add soy sauce.
5. Stir until sauce has a medium consistency. Serve over seafood.*

Yield: 2 cups
Preparation: 15 minutes

*An easy demi-glace to use in or over your favorite seafood or beef dishes. See recipe for dolphin on previous page.

Chef says you can refrigerate sauce and reheat.

FILET OF BEEF MONAGASQUE

A LA - Jean Claude

¼	cup olive oil
8	shallots (chopped)
4	cloves garlic (minced)
4	anchovies (minced)
8	medium tomatoes (peeled and diced)
⅛	t. thyme
40	pitted black olives
1	t. salt
½	t. pepper
1	cup white wine
1	cup veal stock (optional)
8	(6 oz.) fillets of beef
8	T. chopped parsley

1. Heat olive oil in large pan over medium heat.
2. Add shallots, garlic and anchovies. Saute for four minutes.
3. Add tomatoes, thyme, olives, salt and pepper. Cook for four minutes.
4. Add wine and veal stock and simmer.
5. In another pan, brown fillets for two to three minutes on each side. Salt and pepper to taste.
6. Add fillets to sauce and simmer for four minutes. Add parsley.
7. Serve immediately.

Serves: 8
Preparation: 25 minutes

This is a wonderful combination. Try the sauce with other meats.

ORIENTAL DUCK

A LA - Jean Claude

1	**4 - 6 lb. duckling (ready to cook)**
	pepper
4	**slices fresh ginger**
¼	**cup honey**
½	**cup soy sauce**
1	**cup water**
4	**additional slices fresh ginger**

1. Preheat oven to 350°.
2. Rinse and dry inside cavity of duck.
3. Season cavity with pepper and place four slices of ginger inside.
4. Tightly close opening with skewers.
5. Place duck in deep, heavy roasting pan and bake for 1¼ hours.
6. Remove pan from oven; pour off fat.
7. Brush outside of duck with honey.
8. Combine soy sauce and water and pour into bottom of roasting pan.
9. Add remaining ginger slices. Reduce heat to 300° and bake duck until tender. Approximately 1 hour longer.
10. Remove pan from oven; place duck on serving platter and keep warm.
11. Reduce liquid in roasting pan on top of stove until reduced by one half.
12. To serve, cut duck into individual servings and spoon sauce over duck.

Serves: 2 - 4
Preparation: 20 minutes
Cooking time: 2¼ hours

This method complements the duck beautifully. Chicken would also be good cooked this way.

LEG OR SHOULDER OF LAMB STUFFED

A LA - Jean Claude

5 - 6   lb. leg or shoulder of lamb (boned, save bone)
2   T. minced green onions (finely chopped, save peel)
2   shallots (finely chopped, save peel)
3   cloves of garlic (finely chopped, save peel)
½   t. salt
¼   t. pepper
2   cups fresh bread crumbs or 8 slices bread cut into
         pieces
½   cup chopped parsley (finely chopped, save stems)
¼   t. thyme
¼   t. rosemary (minced)
1¼   lb. ground lamb (optional)
1   cup white wine

1.   Preheat oven to 350°. Flatten leg of lamb and break
     bone.
2.   Combine onions, shallots, garlic, salt, pepper, bread
     crumbs, parsley, thyme, rosemary and ground lamb.
3.   Stuff the leg or shoulder by putting mixture down center
     and rolling up. Tie lamb securely.
4.   In lightly oiled roasting pan, brown lamb on all sides on
     top of stove.
5.   Place lamb fat side down. Sprinkle top with salt and
     pepper.
6.   Add bone, peels from onion, shallot, garlic and parsley
     stems.
7.   Bake for 1 - 2 hours until done to your liking. (allow 20 - 30
     minutes per pound, depending on your tastes for rare or
     well done).
8.   Remove from oven; drain fat and remove bone. Place
     lamb on serving platter and keep hot.

— Continued —

9. Add white wine and one cup water to roasting pan and reduce for 4 minutes on top of stove. *
10. To serve, slice meat and pour sauce on top.

Serves: 8
Preparation: 15 minutes
Baking: 1 - 2 hours

* Be sure to stir up particles at bottom of pan and incorporate into the sauce. This is called "deglazing".

This dish is terrific!

MEDALLION D'AGNEAU AUX HERBES
Lamb Chops with Herbs

A LA - Jean Claude

8	small or 4 large lamb chops
1	T. tarragon
½	T. thyme
1	T. black pepper
	cooking twine
2	cups Bearnaise sauce (favorite recipe, or canned or packaged, or see Glossary for recipe)

1. Preheat broiler.
2. Carefully separate fat from meat on chops, still leaving part attached. (See Step 5)
3. Grind together in processor or with mortar and pestle: tarragon, thyme and pepper.
4. Roll meat in the herbs.
5. Bring fat back into place and tie securely with twine.
6. Broil meat until done to your liking - several minutes on each side for medium rare.
7. Serve topped with Bearnaise sauce.

Serves: 4
Preparation: 10 minutes

These chops are succulent and seasoned just right!

RED WINE PEAR
(Prepare ahead and chill until ready to serve)

A LA - Jean Claude

6	**cups red wine**
2½	**cups sugar**
1	**T. cinnamon**
8	**pears**
8	**scoops vanilla ice cream**

1. Combine wine, sugar and cinnamon. Cook over low heat until soft ball stage; on candy thermometer about 234° - 240°.
2. Peel and core pears; but do not remove stems.
3. Add pears to syrup. Cover pan and cook pears until tender yet firm, about fifteen minutes. Remove pears. Chill.
4. Continue cooking sauce until reduced in half. Chill.
5. To serve, place pear and scoop of ice cream on plate; spoon sauce over both and serve.

Serves: 8
Preparation: 1 hour

The flavors are very good together. A lighter dessert.

ST. HONORE SPECIALTY CAKE

Cream Puff Extravaganza
(Begin day before)

A LA - Jean Claude

— Pate Sablee —

½	cup butter (softened)
1½	cups flour
2	T. sugar

— Pate a Choux —

¼	cup butter
1	cup water
1	cup flour
4	eggs (room temperature)

— Cream Mixture —

4	egg yolks
1¼	cups sugar
1	envelope gelatin
2	cups milk (heated to boiling)
2	egg whites (beaten until stiff)
¾	cup cream (whipped)
1	t. vanilla
¼	cup curacao (orange liqueur)

— Caramel —

1	cup sugar
¼	cup water

— Garnish —

¾	cup cream (whipped)

— Continued —

— Pate Sablee —

1. Preheat oven to 325°.
2. Mix butter, flour and sugar together by rubbing dough between your hands until it makes a ball. Roll dough ¼ inch thick and cut a circle 8 inches in diameter.
3. Bake on greased cookie sheet for 20 - 30 minutes until dough turns a sand color. Cool. Set aside on serving platter.

— Pate a Choux —

4. Set oven to 375°.
5. Combine butter and water in saucepan over high heat and bring to a boil. Remove pan from heat and add flour all at once.
6. Stir until dough leaves side of pan and makes a ball.
7. Add eggs, one at a time, beating well after each. Dough will become smooth and shiny.
8. Place dough in pastry bag and, on ungreased cookie sheets, pipe two 8-inch rings and 18 medium sized cream puffs. Bake in oven 24 minutes or until puffy, golden and dry. Remove and cool.

— Cream Mixture —

9. Combine egg yolks, sugar and gelatin. Beat together on low speed for 5 minutes.
10. Continue beating and slowly add boiling milk.
11. Pour into saucepan and cook slowly until mixture turns creamy so that it coats a spoon. DO NOT BOIL.
12. Cool and refrigerate until mixture starts to gel.
13. Fold in: Stiff egg whites, whipped cream, vanilla and curacao.
14. Refrigerate while assembling shell.

— Continued —

— Caramel —

15. Combine water and sugar in saucepan and cook until it turns an amber color.
16. Using caramel as paste, stick 2 Pate a Choux rings on top of each other, on top of the Pate Sablee base.
17. Then stick cream puffs on top of final ring. Pour remaining Caramel on top and down sides of shell.
18. Fill shell with Cream Mixture and let set in refrigerator for 4 hours.
19. Serve with whipped cream on top.

Serves: 8
Preparation: 3 hours
Refrigeration: 3 hours

A festive finale to any occasion! Guaranteed to be a hit!

APRICOT SOUFFLE
(Marinate apricots overnight, so start day ahead)

A LA - Jean Claude

1	**12 oz. can apricots with syrup**
¼	**cup apricot liqueur of your choice**
1	**8 oz. package dried apricots (finely chopped)**
8	**egg whites (room temperature)**
	dash cream of tartar
	butter (to coat dish)
	sugar (to coat dish)

1. Marinate canned apricots and their syrup in liqueur overnight. Drain, reserving both syrup and fruit.
2. Add one half cup water to reserved syrup. In a large pan cook liquids to soft ball stage, 240° (syrup will be thick).*
3. Add reserved fruit and chopped dried apricots; bring to a boil. Cool.
4. Preheat oven to 275°.
5. Beat egg whites and cream of tartar until stiff. Pour in fruit while still beating at low speed.
6. Pour into buttered and sugared souffle dish.
7. Bake for 45 minutes.

Serves: 6-8
Preparation: 45 minutes
Baking: 45 minutes
Marinate: overnight

* If you do not have a candy thermometer, drop a small quantity of syrup in ice water. Syrup will form a flattened ball when ready.

This easy dish is very delicious and light. A perfect summer dessert.

CHARLOTTE DE POMME
Apple Charlotte Dessert

A LA - Jean Claude

12	slices regular white bread (crust removed)
12	apples (peeled and finely diced)
4	T. butter
1½	cups sugar
¼	cup rum
1 ·	T. vanilla
	pinch of cinnamon
2	cups apricot sauce or preserves (heated)

1. Preheat oven to 325°.
2. Slice bread in half and into thin rectangles. Dry bread in a saute pan over medium heat until golden brown. Line a buttered mold or 3 quart pan with the bread.
3. Saute apples and butter together until all moisture is gone and you have a dry puree.
4. Add sugar, rum, vanilla and cinnamon. Mix together well.
5. Fill the bread-lined mold with apple puree.
6. Bake for 35 minutes in middle of oven.
7. Meanwhile, in separate pan, heat sauce or preserves. Keep hot.
8. Remove apple dish from oven. Top with sauce and serve warm.

Serves 6-8
Preparation: 25 minutes
Baking: 35 minutes

A lighter dessert that my family really enjoyed!

FROM WILD MUSTANGS TO CHARDONNAY

Because the improvement and greater variety of American wines have played a major role in the increased attention given American cuisine, it seems only proper to discuss the massive effort now underway in Texas to make the state's wine industry both nationally and internationally competitive.

The growing of grapes and the making of wine is not new to Texas. The earliest explorers found the native Wild Mustang Grape growing profusely within her borders. One hundred years before Father Serra brought the Mission Grape to California, Spanish missionaries introduced winemaking at the Ysleta Mission near El Paso in 1662. Viticulturists, experts in the growing of grapes, have long regarded Texas as a natural home for the grape due to the state's ideal soil and favorable climate.

From 1880 until the advent of Texas Prohibition in 1919, many small wineries dotted the Texas landscape. With Prohibition however, their demise was swift, complete and with one exception, lasted forty years beyond Repeal in 1933.

If there be any notion the present vinous movement is of momentary fancy and short duration, put such thoughts to rest. Texas' recent grape harvests are the result of high level discussions, extensive planning and exhaustive research commenced in the late 1960's. The force behind this long range effort is the University of Texas, said by some to be the wealthiest institution of higher learning in the world, source of scientists capable of extracting the best the grape can provide and owner of hundreds of thousands of acres in West Texas. This vast acreage, some used for little more than grazing, coupled with improvements in drip irrigation led the university to consider the grape.

Other Texas universities have also been involved. Since 1976, Texas Tech, in cooperation with the University of Texas, has

— Continued —

engaged in wine research. Texas A&M, with its Agricultural-Experimental Stations and Extension Services, has also been studying the problems associated with the growing of grapes and the making of wine.

The quality of the grapes and wine under discussion is strictly premium. We are speaking primarily of the Vitis-vinifera, the prized European varietal grapes and hybrids. At this time, Chardonnay, Johannesburg Reisling, Cabernet Sauvingnon and Pinot Noir grapes are only some of the vinifera group that are producing successful harvests in Texas.

In contrast to California's 350,000 acres devoted to grapes, Texas, while having just scratched the surface, sees a future potential of almost one million productive acres. In the not-too-distant future, Texas predicts it will be second only to California in total U.S. wine production.

The success already realized from the painstaking and diligent groundwork should not be understated. With initial harvests less than eight years off the vine, some blind-taste tests have already placed some moderately priced Texas varietals ahead of their California counterparts. Additionally, both in-state and out-of-state competitions increasingly recognize Texas vintners. Available for purchase at some wineries and in various retail stores, Texas wines are now being found in some of the state's finest restaurants. Austin's Green Pastures has gone one step further by converting second floor quarters into "The Texas Wine Room".

Should any of this be thought a case of Texas' blind love for anything Texan, please note several foreign countries are also involved. Cordier of Bordeaux, France, that country's leading exporter of wines and spirits, has staked a claim under the partnership, Gill Richter Cordier. The Richter connection is Richter S.A., one of the world's leading viticultural nurseries located in Montpellier, France. Also, California wine interests have been warming seats at Texas legislative sessions while lobbying for revisions in a Texas law that presently limits non-resident participation.

— Continued —

As of 1985 there are approximately fifteen licensed wineries in the state of Texas with more on the horizon. Several of these enterprises are somewhat isolated as is the case of Gill Richter Cordier and the one-hundred-year-old Val Verde operation in Del Rio. However, a number of wineries are more accessible in North Central, Central and South Central Texas. Most of these wineries are open to the public; some in addition to having tasting rooms, offer their product for sale.

All this leads to a suggestion you may wish to consider. There is no better way to enjoy Texas countryside and learn of wine-making than by visiting one or several of these wineries. After calling to confirm visiting hours and location, leave the hotel or home and with a map and directions in hand, put the city behind you. As of this writing, there are six wineries, each within several hours of Austin and San Antonio; two within an easy drive of Forth Worth and two near Lubbock. Because some of these operations are open only on a limited basis, we stress the importance of calling ahead.

On a bright morning in March, I drove west from Austin for an appointment with Dale and Penny Bettis of the Cypress Valley Winery. While the subject of grapes sent me, this was The Hill Country and I knew it provided more than grapes. Set in its folds are lakes, rivers, streams, abandoned quarries and caves. There are deer, fox, bobcat, armadillo, wild turkey and red-tailed hawk. Blue on pink vistas are broken with pine, juniper, oak, mesquite and sage. Quiet country roads turn and dip to nature's paintbrush then rise to nourish a post office, gas station and grocery store - a town - all neatly arranged in a former school house.

A wrong turn resulted in my late arrival beside an impressive nineteenth century home of stone and one of the Bettis' several vineyards. March begins the growing season, so after introductions, Penny returned to her pruning shears while Dale and I drove their truck to more distant plantings. Enroute, I learned the importance of drip irrigation, a technique dis-covered by Americans and perfected by the Israelis. I heard of T.V. Munson, a grape breeder from Denison, Texas who in the

— Continued —

1880's helped save the French wine industry from a devastating blight. Munson is something of a folk hero among Texan vintners and provides that French connection. Returning from the vineyards, we visited the winery, a converted garage which now contained a stemmer, crusher, fermentation tanks and casks made of French and Missouri oak. Finally, we stepped into the Tasting Room and Dale poured me a glass of Cypress Valley Chenin Blanc. My senses rose to the occasion as this man of many talents concluded his presentation by saying that the Texas wine industry has reached a point where it knows it can compete; it is now a matter of applying proper marketing techniques and time.

Listed below are nine wineries near Austin, Fort Worth, Lubbock and San Antonio with our last entry a deserved salute to the Qualia Family's one-hundred-year-old operation in Del Rio. Just as the grape is drawing life from the plains, plateaus and hills of Texas, so too can a human spirit suffering life's periodic stupors.

AUSTIN

Cypress Valley Winery
Cypress Mill, Texas
(512) 825-3333
Hours: Sat., 10-6;
Sun., Noon-6
Winery and vineyards
On-premise sales

Fall Creek Vineyards
Tow, Texas
(915) 379-5361
Hours: Last Sat. of each month,
1-5 p.m.
Winery and vineyards
No sales on premises

FORT WORTH

La Buena Vida Vineyards
Springtown, Texas
(817) 237-9463
Hours: Daily,
by appointment only
Winery and vineyards
On-premise sales

Chateau Montgolfier
Vineyards
P.O. Box 12423
Fort Worth, Texas
(817) 448-8479
Call for appointment
Winery and vineyard
No sales on premises

— Continued —

LUBBOCK

Llano Estacado Winery
Lubbock, Texas
(806) 745-2258
Hours: Sat., Noon-6;
Sun., 1:30-6
Winery and vineyards
On-premise sales

Pheasant Ridge Winery
Lubbock, Texas
(806) 793-4413
Call for appointment
Winery and vineyard
No sales on premises

SAN ANTONIO

Guadalupe Valley Winery
New Braunfels, Texas
(512) 629-2351
Hours:
    Tours: Sat. & Sun., 1-4
    Tasting Room: Mon. thru Sat.,
    10 a.m.-; Sun., Noon-
Winery only
On-premise sales

Moyer Texas Champagne Co.
New Braunfels, Texas
(512) 625-5181
Hours: Mon.-Sat., 10-5
Winery only
On-premise sales

Oberhellmann Vineyards
Fredericksburg, Texas
(512) 685-3297
Group appointments only
Winery and vineyards

DEL RIO

Val Verde Winery
139 Hudson Drive
Del Rio, Texas
(512) 775-9714
Hours: Mon. - Sat., 9-5
Winery and vineyard
On-premise sales

Remember to call ahead and verify visiting hours.

WINE TOUR NOTES

CONCLUSION
Visit Texas' Rich Heritage

Years ago, textbooks, television and song introduced me to Houston, Crockett, the Red River, the Rio Grande, Abilene and San Antonio. In fact, Texas has been the object of such prolonged and broad media exposure that many of us feel that we know her on something more than a casual basis.

Her story is one of high drama set in a land that beautifully orchestrates color and vista. A story that can compete with any state and surpass most. A multi-faceted saga of varying terrain, climates, cultures, industry, architecture and heroic people. Therefore, while in Texas, some attempt should be made to achieve a greater familiarization with her past and present.

San Antonio provides the best single opportunity to investigate Texas' rich heritage. This sun-drenched city with heavy Hispanic leanings is the crucible of Texas liberty, the home of five Spanish missions including the Alamo, the Spanish Governor's Palace, San Fernando Cathedral and the Institute of Texas Cultures.

I chose to begin my investigations by driving to the southern edge of San Antonio and visiting Mission Espada. Established more than one-hundred years before Texas independence, this mission and her sister missions shaped and directed the lives of native Texans until the very early nineteenth century.

Along the road connecting the five missions, one will discover the Espada Aquaduct, the Espada Dam and remnants of Spanish irrigation systems. All are approximately 250 years old and the aquaduct and dam are still operative.

The last mission I visited was the first to be built along the banks of the San Antonio River in 1718. Originally named San Antonio de Valero, this mission gained its greatest fame after its abandonment by the church and under its more popular name, The Alamo.

— Continued —

Ordered destroyed by Houston, bombarded and breached by Santa Anna, pushed to the point of collapse by urban development, the Alamo now seems to be holding its own quite well. While a cinematic re-creation of its fall seems barely adequate, I found the Alamo a pleasant surprise and surveyed its contents on two separate occasions.

Galveston and Galveston Island are named in honor of Bernardo de Galvez, Spanish Governor of Louisiana during the American Revolutionary War. Discovered by Spanish explorers in the early sixteenth century, Galveston Island is the probable site of Cabeza de Vaca's shipwreck in 1528. "Los Naufragious", the chronicle of his seven years of subsequent wanderings and capture, may be the first book on Texas. Later, the island was visited and occupied by Indians, adventurers, revolutionists and buccaneers.

Galveston is the home of oleander, bougainvillaea, stately Victorian residences, a one-hundred year old sailing ship and a ten-mile seawall erected after the tidal wave of 1900 devastated the city and killed 6,000 persons.

Fishing and shrimping fleets anchor here and shipbuilding is an island industry. From atop the Coast Guard station, Petty Officer Jack Robinson of Killeen, Texas, identified a Russian freighter, a school of porpoise and the 24-hour ferry that takes cars and passengers, free of charge, from Galveston Island across the mouth of Galveston Bay to the Bolivar Peninsula..

For those who enjoy the mountains, desert and solitude, Big Bend National Park offers almost 1100 square miles in which to wander. From the floor of the Chihauhaun Desert rise the Chisos and Dead Horse Mountains to altitudes approaching 8000 feet. Within the park's three major canyons grow Mexican pinyon, oak, aspen, pine, big-tooth maple, Texas Madrone, greasewood and spiny ocotillo. To further brighten the surroundings, there are over 400 species of birds including the Lucifer Hummingbird and the Colima Warbler, the latter found nowhere else in this country.

A good sampling of Texas' natural and social history lies in the

— Continued —

very accessible Hill Country of South Central Texas. Fredericksburg, located approximately eighty miles west of Austin, is delightfully steeped in German traditions and nineteenth century architecture. German festivals and cuisine, the Nimitz Hotel and the Pioneer Museum have drawn visitors from across the country.

Moving east along Route 290, the beautiful Pedernales River courses its way past the Lyndon B. Johnson State Historical Park and the LBJ Ranch. The former offers colorful slide shows, a variety of exhibits and a working replica of a nineteenth century farm. From the park a bus will take you on a free tour of the LBJ Ranch. The tour is very scenic, informative and provides a rather comprehensive look at the native haunts and home-life of our 36th president.

Further east along Route 290 lies Johnson City and LBJ's boyhood home. The modest, yet attractive structure provides a nostalgic look into a family life that seems laced with love, discipline and beautiful simplicity. From here, a horse-drawn wagon will take you to the Johnson Settlement, a cluster of restored structures which trace the evolution of the Hill Country from open range to more recent times.

East of Johnson City lies Pedernales State Park. Here is an opportunity to hike a variety of trails, view dense stands of pine, see sculptured canyons and contemplate the Pedernales winding over natural rock dams, around sandstone outcroppings, making her way to the Colorado River.

If rocks, dust and adobe do not suit you, perhaps the Dallas-Fort Worth area will prove more to your liking. Some say Dallas may be the most culturally oriented city in North America. Dallas boasts an opera, symphony, ballet, Shakespearean festival, civic chorus, summer musicals and a sixty-square-acre art complex including the recently opened Museum of Art.

However, Dallas does not stand alone with regards to cultural possessions. Less than one hour west lie Fort Worth's wonderful boulevards, parks, zoo, world-class Botanic Gardens, art col-

— Continued —

lections and historic landmarks including the Fort Worth Stockyards National Historic District.

It should be no surprise that a city of beautiful parks and boulevards also has a most creditable collection of art. The Amon Carter Museum, the Kimball Museum and the Fort Worth Art Museum all deserve your inspection. The Amon Carter Museum of American Art features some of the best works of George Caleb Bingham, Frederic-Remington, Charles Russell, Georgia O'Keefe, Winslow Homer and Alfred Miller. One painting alone is worth driving miles to see. Thomas Cole's "The Hunter's Return" is a much heralded acquisition whose color and majesty is as fine an example of the Hudson River School as any painting hanging east of the Monongahela.

Perhaps it is most appropriate to end our trek through Texas on the eastern outskirts of Houston, at the San Jacinto Memorial. There, on April 21, 1836, an engagement between the forces of Sam Houston and Santa Anna freed Texas of Mexican rule and led to the eventual annexation of Texas as well as much of our western United States.

Directly beneath the 570 foot monument is a fine museum containing numerous displays that detail Texas history in the early nineteenth century. Impressions of Houston and Austin are clarified via their letters, some photographs and other personal possessions.

Tools of work and war put flesh and bones on sometimes vague impressions of prairie farmers, ranchers and citizen soldiers.

Outside, encircling the monument's base is grassy bottom-land, live oak and etched in the monuments limestone walls a record of events surrounding this famous battle. The displays, inscriptions and terrain all serve to resusitate a cause, bring forgotten and unknown heroes to the fore and reconstitute the emotions that drove such men as Colonel Edward Stiff to pen an invitation that defies improvement and provides an apt conclusion to these endeavors.

— Continued —

"To the young and vigorous who must be the architects of their own fortune. . . to those who are doomed by the customs of densely populated places to be mere hewers of wood and drawers of water, to the hitherto imprudent, to the unfortunate, to the discarded from society; I emphatically say to all such, Go, and go at once, to Texas!"

MICHAEL C. GRADY

GLOSSARY OF TERMS

Al Dente

Cooked until tender but not soft; 5 - 10 minutes. Home-made noodles, 5 minutes; if on shelf for long period, 8 - 10 minutes. Literally in Italian this means "to the tooth". In other words, it resists your bite slightly.

Bearnaise Sauce

This is a Hollandaise Sauce flavored with Tarragon, Shallots and Wine. You can add those ingredients to your Hollandaise or follow the recipe here:

5 egg yolks (large) 3 T. lemon juice, salt and pepper to taste, 3 T. shallots (minced) 2 T. wine vinegar, 1½ T. dried tarragon, 1½ cups butter (melted) ¼ t. tabasco - Combine yolks, lemon juice and salt and pepper in top of double boiler over gently simmering water. Whip together with whisk until sauce begins to thicken. In separate pan, simmer shallots, vinegar and tarragon for three minutes. Slowly add to yolk mixture. Reduce heat and very slowly add melted butter, drop by drop, all the while beating the sauce with electric beater until sauce is consistency of Hollandaise. Finally, add tabasco.

Bordelaise Sauce

Prepare the same way you do BROWN SAUCE except in addition to the onion, saute also ½ carrot (sliced), a few slices of celery, a sprig of parsley and ½ bay leaf (crushed). Add 1 T. of ketchup or tomato puree and if you desire, a dash of worcestershire and dry red wine. If you use packaged gravy, simply add 1 T. catsup and a dash of worcestershire sauce.

Brown Sauce

You may use packaged Beef Gravy Sauce or make your own. The following is a very simple recipe using ingredients you most likely have on hand:

Saute 1 T. of diced onion in 2 T. of butter. Add 2 T. flour to make a roux. Stir in 1 cup of consomme or beef bouillon and salt and pepper to taste. Cook over low heat, stirring constantly, or cook in a double boiler. Strain. Yields 1 cup.

Butterfly

To Butterfly Shrimp: Remove shell but leave tail intact. Devein. Turn upside down and cut all the way down length of shrimp to tail and almost all the way through to other side. (leave about 1/16

— Continued —

inch to act as a hinge). Spread shrimp open butterfly fashion and lay flat. It will resemble the shape of a butterfly.

For other meats: Slicing against or across the grain to make it more tender. Also, to open up a pocket for stuffing by cutting through the middle of the side of a filet and opening up two flaps which can later enclose stuffing.

Clarified, Clarify

To make clear by adding a clarifying agent or removing sediment. In the case of butter, simply melt it over low heat. In between the foam on top and the milk solids which will have settled to the bottom of your pan, you will have a clear liquid. This is your clarified butter. Skim the foam from the top and discard. Tilt pan to gather your clarified butter. The sediment at the bottom can be discarded or used in baking if you desire.

Creme Fraiche

To make this slightly soured cream, you add 1 T. buttermilk to 1 cup heavy cream. Let sit in warm place overnight - or about 15 - 20 hours. In some cases you may substitute heavy cream.

Correct the Seasonings

Add salt and pepper to taste.

Demi-Glace

A reduced Brown Sauce. For a quick Demi-Glace, simply cook brown gravy 15 - 20 minutes until flavors are concentrated. You can use a packaged gravy.

Deglaze

To moisten a roast pan or saute pan with wine, vinegar, stock or water in order to dissolve the carmelized drippings from roasted meats, etc., so that they might be used in the sauce. To do this, scrape up the bottom residue into the liquid with a wooden spatula while cooking over low heat.

Dressed

Stuffed.

Fish Stock

Add ½ cup each of sliced onion, carrot and celery to 3 cups cold water and ½ cup white wine. Bring to a boil and add 1 lb. of fish bones, head, tails, trimmings, etc. Cook for twenty minutes and strain. In some cases you may substitute chicken stock or bouillon.

— Continued —

281

Flamber or Flambe

> This process adds flavor to dessert and meat dishes. Light match to warmed liqueur to make a flame and burn off the alcohol. It's easy to ignite if you tilt the pan and touch the flame to the edge. It will burn itself out.

Flour (Browned)

> This is great for gravies and sauce as it enhances the flavor. Simply brown the amount of flour you need in a cast iron skillet or other heavy pan, stirring constantly. Be sure the flour does not get too brown. It should be golden brown in color. An alternate method is to brown it in a moderate oven for 20 - 30 minutes till golden, stirring occasionally.

Garlic (Pressed)

> Use a garlic press to squeeze out the juice and pulverize the clove. Discard the hull. If you do not own a press, you may mash the garlic with the blade of a knife or with the back of a spoon against the side of the bowl you are using.

Ignite

> See Flamber

Julienne

> To cut in long thin 1½ inch strips. Should be thinner than French fries.

Lump Crab Meat

> Lump crab meat or back-fin meat is taken from the body of the blue crabs. It is white in color. You may use just about any kind of crab for most of the recipes included in this book. While doing so, however, it's interesting to keep notes on the difference in color, taste and even the texture. Claw meat, for example, is harder to shell and is brownish in color but is very tasty.

Puff Pastry

> A light puffy pastry dough. Since this requires a lot of time and perfect conditions to make, we suggest you purchase it in your grocer's bakery section. It's best to go in early or call the day before and reserve some. You can also use frozen dough for puff pastries such as croissant dough. After the dough has reached room temperature, roll it into flat rectangular shape as called for in the recipes of this book.

— Continued —

Reduce

To reduce the quantity of a liquid by simmering. This makes a stock or sauce more flavorful because it's more concentrated and is thickened.

Roux

Equal parts of flour and butter cooked - used to thicken sauces and gravies. (Melt butter over low heat. Stir in flour and cook over low heat for 1 - 2 minutes, until mixture is thick and well blended).

Saute

To cook quickly in small amount of fat or butter.

Seasonings

(Adjust or Correct) To make sure seasonings (salt and pepper, etc.) are correct to the taste - your taste. Add more if necessary.

Shuck

(Noun) - A husk, shell or pod. A shell of an oyster or clam. (Verb) - To remove shell of oyster or clam. You can do this by prying shell hinge open with knife and then inserting knife all around edge or place shells in hot oven for 5 minutes and drop in ice bath. Drain. Shells will open.

Sweetbreads

The pancreas of beef and veal. Use veal sweetbreads in all the recipes in this book. Make sure they are very fresh.

Vinaigrette Dressing Recipe

The proportions are usually 4 parts oil to 1 part lemon or lime juice or vinegar. Add herbs, spices and seasonings as you like. Here is one version: 1 tsp. salt, pinch of paprika, pinch of dry mustard, 2 T. vinegar, 8 T. olive oil, pinch of fresh ground pepper and ¼ tsp. of chopped parsley. Mix together thoroughly and serve.

Zest

The grated peelings from citrus fruits which add wonderful flavors. Avoid the white portion attached to the peel as it is bitter.

CATEGORY INDEX

Exact Recipe Titles Under Course Categories.
General Recipe Index follows Category Index

APPETIZERS AND HORS D'OEUVRES

(Several Entrees can also be used as Appetizers - See Entrees)

SALADS

SOUPS

284

CATEGORY INDEX — Continued

CATEGORY INDEX — Continued

— Continued —

CATEGORY INDEX — Continued

— Continued —

CATEGORY INDEX — Continued

GENERAL RECIPE INDEX

A Listing of Every Recipe by Category and Major Ingredient

— **Continued** —

GENERAL RECIPE INDEX — Continued

— Continued —

GENERAL RECIPE INDEX — Continued

— Continued —

GENERAL RECIPE INDEX — Continued

— Continued —

292

GENERAL RECIPE INDEX — Continued

— Continued —

293

GENERAL RECIPE INDEX — Continued

— Continued —

GENERAL RECIPE INDEX — Continued

— Continued —

GENERAL RECIPE INDEX — Continued

— Continued —

GENERAL RECIPE INDEX — Continued

— Continued —

GENERAL RECIPE INDEX — Continued

— Continued —

GENERAL RECIPE INDEX — Continued

— Continued —

GENERAL RECIPE INDEX — Continued

Dear Friends,

Would you like us to send you other books in our series? Or send them as gift(s) to your friend(s)? We mail promptly and guarantee satisfaction!

Thank you for your order, and remember, we always appreciate your comments.

Catherine Grady Crabtree

FREE SHIPPING ON FOUR BOOKS OR MORE!

Qty.	Title	Unit Price		Shipping	Total
	A LA NEW ORLEANS	$ 9.95	soft cover	$1.00 ea.	
	A LA SAN FRANCISCO	$ 9.95	soft cover	$1.00 ea.	
	A LA ASPEN	$ 9.95	soft cover	$1.00 ea.	
	A LA TEXAS	$14.95	hard cover	$1.50 ea.	
		(PRICES SUBJECT TO CHANGE)	TOTAL ENCLOSED		

Name_____

Address_____

City_____ State_____ Zip_____

☐ This is a gift. Send directly to: ☐ Please gift wrap (no charge)

Name_____

Address_____

City_____ State_____ Zip_____

(Help us serve you better. Please fill out reverse side)

Crabtree Publishing
P.O. Box 3451
Federal Way, WA 98003

Dear Friends,

Would you like us to send you other books in our series? Or send them as gift(s) to your friend(s)? We mail promptly and guarantee satisfaction!

Thank you for your order, and remember, we always appreciate your comments.

Catherine Grady Crabtree

FREE SHIPPING ON FOUR BOOKS OR MORE!

Qty.	Title	Unit Price		Shipping	Total
	A LA NEW ORLEANS	$ 9.95	soft cover	$1.00 ea.	
	A LA SAN FRANCISCO	$ 9.95	soft cover	$1.00 ea.	
	A LA ASPEN	$ 9.95	soft cover	$1.00 ea.	
	A LA TEXAS	$14.95	hard cover	$1.50 ea.	
		(PRICES SUBJECT TO CHANGE)		TOTAL ENCLOSED	

Name_____

Address_____

City_____ State_____ Zip_____

☐ This is a gift. Send directly to: ☐ Please gift wrap (no charge)

Name_____

Address_____

City_____ State_____ Zip_____

(Help us serve you better. Please fill out reverse side)

Crabtree Publishing
P.O. Box 3451
Federal Way, WA 98003

303

Dear Friends,

Would you like us to send you other books in our series? Or send them as gift(s) to your friend(s)? We mail promptly and guarantee satisfaction!

Thank you for your order, and remember, we always appreciate your comments.

Catherine Grady Crabtree

FREE SHIPPING ON FOUR BOOKS OR MORE!

Qty.	Title	Unit Price		Shipping	Total
	A LA NEW ORLEANS	$ 9.95	soft cover	$1.00 ea.	
	A LA SAN FRANCISCO	$ 9.95	soft cover	$1.00 ea.	
	A LA ASPEN	$ 9.95	soft cover	$1.00 ea.	
	A LA TEXAS	$14.95	hard cover	$1.50 ea.	
		(PRICES SUBJECT TO CHANGE)		TOTAL ENCLOSED	

Name_____

Address_____

City_____ State_____ Zip_____

☐ This is a gift. Send directly to:　　☐ Please gift wrap (no charge)

Name_____

Address_____

City_____ State_____ Zip_____

(Help us serve you better. Please fill out reverse side)

Crabtree Publishing
P.O. Box 3451
Federal Way, WA 98003

305